Indiana's Timeless Tales - 1792 – 1794

The Northwest Indian War

Indiana History Time Line Series – Book 3

Paul R. Wonning

Indiana's Timeless Tales - 1792 – 1794
Published By Paul R. Wonning
Copyright 2017 by Paul R. Wonning
Print Edition

mossyfeetbooks@gmail.com

If you would like email notification of when new Mossy Feet books become available email the author for inclusion in the subscription list.

Mossy Feet Books
www.mossyfeetbooks.com

Indiana Places

http://indianaplaces.blogspot.com/

Description

Explore Indiana's early history using this journal of history stories from the beginning days of the Northwest Territory. A Timeline of Indiana History - 1792 - 1794 relates the time line of events that occurred between St. Clair's Defeat to, and including the Battles of Fort Recovery and Fallen Timbers. Many of these stories of the Northwest Indian War are little known and obscure historical tales that the reader will enjoy learning.

Table of Contents

January 1795 - Native Leaders Gather at Fort Greenville

Also In This Series

January 1792

January 01, 1792 - Early Indiana

In early 1792, the region that would become Indiana consisted of land claimed by the various Indian tribes that lived in the dense forests, swamps and prairies, traveling and using the fishes of the rivers and streams as a valuable food source.

Settlements

In 1792, only three settlements existed in the future state, Vincennes, Clarksville and Jeffersonville. Cincinnati, located in the southwest corner of the future state of Ohio served as capital of the Northwest Territory. All of these settlements lay along major rivers.

Northwest Territory

Major John Hamtramck commanded Fort Knox I at Vincennes, constructed in 1787, was the westernmost fort of the United States. Arthur St. Clair governor of the Northwest Territory, which included the lands comprising the future states of Ohio, Indiana, Illinois, Michigan, Wisconsin and a portion of Minnesota.

Settlement

The great cost of waging the Revolutionary War had left the government of the United States with an almost overwhelming debt that the new nation could not pay. The lands of the Northwest Territory beckoned, providing a means of paying the soldiers that fought the war. The United States granted land to Revolutionary War veterans, who began moving into the areas north of the Ohio River granted to them. The land also provided a much needed cash flow medium, as the government could have tracts of land surveyed and sold off to the public. The government established land offices for people to buy this land. These people also moved into their new holdings, many of which were north of the Ohio River. Amerindian tribes that lived in the region saw these new settlers as a threat to their way of life. They also viewed them as a violation Treaty of Fort Stanwix, signed in 1768, that set the border between the whites and the Amerindians at the Ohio River. The United States, with great reluctance, created an army to deal with the threat. However, the government did not give this early army the resources it needed to succeed. This policy led to the disasters of General Harmar in 1790 and St. Clair's Defeat (Battle of the Wabash) in 1791. After the disastrous Battle of the Wabash, the United States set out on a different course to enlarge its settled territory.

January 24, 1792 - Wilkinson Departs for Fort Jefferson

Lieutenant Colonel James Wilkinson had assumed temporary command of the Second Regiment in December 1791 stationed at Fort Washington when General Arthur St. Clair departed for Philadelphia. St Clair had departed to report on the disaster that had befallen his army on November 4, 1791.

Bury the Dead and Attack

Wilkinson's mission had four main objectives:

Provide supplies for the desperate troops stationed at Fort Jefferson

Visit the battlefield and bury the dead

Recover cannon and other valuable supplies left on the battlefield

Attack an Indian village fifteen miles from the battlefield, which was on the banks of a tributary of the Wabash River.

Earlier in the month, Wilkinson had issued a call for 150 volunteers for the mission. The required number of men had responded and Wilkinson readied his force, which would be composed of the 150 volunteers and about 50 regular troops. Future Indiana Territorial Governor William Henry Harrison served as an ensign during this mission.

Departure

Wilkinson departed Fort Washington during a cold snap that had frozen the Ohio River. Snow two feet deep covered the ground and progress was slow, as the cavalry had to clear the way with their horses for the infantry that followed.

Major David Ziegler had led an earlier relief mission in December 1791. He encountered 116 starving survivors. To survive, these men ate horsemeat and hides. Ziegler left supplies for them and returned to Fort Washington.

January 30, 1792 - Lieutenant Colonel James Wilkinson Relief Mission Arrives Fort Jefferson

Traveling by the route cut earlier by St. Clair's troops in preparation for their November mission, Wilkinson's force completed the seventy-mile journey on January 30.

Starving Troops

They arrived at the fort on January 30, finding the troops that remained there in a sorry state. The bitter cold weather prevented him from carrying out his plan to raid the Indian village, so he sent the infantry back to Fort Washington and departed for the battle site to bury the dead and recover the cannon the army had left behind during the retreat.

February 1792

February 01, 1792 - Wilkinson Arrives at the Battle Site

The soldiers began encountering bodies in the snow along the trail, beginning where the Indians had stopped their pursuit of the fleeing army. On the way to the battleground, they counted seventy-eight bodies. Cold temperatures and snow had set in right after the battle, so there had been little decomposition, however they were not able to identify many due to the fact that the warriors had scalped, stripped and mutilated the bodies as well as damage inflicted by scavenging animals. The bodies, covered in snow and frozen to the ground, were difficult to move to the mass grave site. They did find one body they thought was General Richard Butler. Since they had not brought enough shovels for all the men, they dug one large pit and piled all the bodies in it. The number of bodies, around 600, created a huge mound of dirt when they covered them. The warriors had dismounted the cannon and the carriages had mostly been destroyed by fire or otherwise damaged.

After burying as many bodies as they could find, the army returned to Fort Washington.

February 11, 1792 - Indians Attack Hunting Party at Fort Jefferson

Captain Joseph Shaylor, commander of Fort Jefferson, had taken his twelve year old son, Joseph, and a few soldiers on a hunting expedition on February 11, 1791. A band of Indians attacked the hunting party, killing his son and a civilian military contractor. Shaylor was wounded in the incident.

Joseph Shaylor (October 23, 1746 - March 04, 1816)

The son of Joseph and Mary Fowler Shaylor, Joseph was native to Haddam, Middlesex County, Connecticut. Shaylor

4

enlisted in the Connecticut State Infantry Regiment on June 20, 1776. Shaylor saw extensive action during the Revolutionary War, rising from ensign to lieutenant until his discharge on November 15, 1783. He reentered the military on March 14, 1791 when he received appointment as a captain in the Second United States Regiment of Infantry to recruit soldiers for duty in the Northwest Indian Wars.

Deployment to Fort Washington

Shaylor's company first assignment was to the Perth Amboy and Brunsworth Barracks where they stayed until they began the march to Fort Pitt on May 31. After arriving at Fort Pitt the company floated down the Ohio to join the garrison at Fort Harmar. On In late August his company joined Captain Newman's party on his journey to Fort Washington. They arrived on September 10.

Commander of Fort Jefferson

On October 24, 1791, General St. Clair placed him in command of Fort Jefferson while he and the remainder of the army went on to defeat a few days later. Shaylor and his company provided shelter and what medicinal care they could offer to the wounded survivors of the battle. Shaylor completed the construction of Fort Jefferson.

Indians Attack Hunting Party at Fort Jefferson

Captain Joseph Shaylor, commander of Fort Jefferson, had taken his twelve year old son, Joseph, and a few soldiers on a hunting expedition on February 11, 1791. A band of Indians attacked the hunting party, killing his son and a civilian military contractor. Shaylor was wounded in the incident.

Relieved of Command

General Wilkinson relieved Shaylor of his command on February 28 and court martial him for hazarding his command in March. Wilkinson relieved him of command for six months.

Natives Attack Supply Wagon Convoy

A small band of Indian warriors attacked a twenty wagon supply convoy just as it crossed Seven Mile Creek a short distance north of Fort. St. Clair. The attackers killed twelve privates and one officer. There were seven men missing in action after the attack. The Indians captured the entire lead herd of seventy horses, leaving the wagons and supplies on them in the middle of the road. The loss of the horses proved troublesome for the contractor charged with bringing supplies into the camp. Joseph Shaylor, court-martialed by General James Wilkinson, had been reinstated by General Anthony Wayne, who had placed him in command of Fort St. Clair. Shaylor had been in command of one of the columns in the convoy, on the way to Wayne's camp.

March 1792

March 05, 1794 - Congress Approves Act Creating the Legion of the United States

The defeat inflicted upon St. Claire's army in November 1792 spurred Congress into authorizing President Washington to increase the size and organization of the army.

Three Additional Regiments

The Act authorized President Washington to recruit three additional infantry regiments and a squadron of dragoons. It also gave him the authority to complete recruiting and organizing two of the infantry regiments and one artillery regiment then in existence. It also gave Washington the authority to reorganize the army, adding or reducing the size as he and the Secretary of War Henry Knox saw fit. Washington and Knox favored the legion form advocated by Baron Friedrich Wilhelm von Steuben.

Legion of the United States

Congress approved the reorganized Army under the name of the Legion of the United States. United States leaders of this era admired the early Roman republic and chose the name Legion to honor that republic. The Legion would have four sub-legions of 1280 men each, commanded by a brigadier general. It would have two battalions of infantry, one battalion of riflemen, one company of artillery and one company of dragoons. A company was the basic military unit and usually consisted of 80 to 250 soldiers commanded by a major or a captain. The battalion was a combination of several companies and consists of between 300 and 800 soldiers, commanded by a lieutenant colonel. The Congress authorized the creation of the rank of major general to command the new Legion. President Washington examined several candidates and chose Revolutionary War hero Anthony Wayne to lead this new Army.

Dragoon

Dragoons were a form of mounted infantry that had the mobility of cavalry; however they fought on foot like infantry troops. A company of dragoons offered mobility to an army in the field, allowing commanders to move companies of dragoons quickly around the battlefield as needed.

Baron von Steuben (September 17, 1730 - November 28, 1794)

The Baron's full birth name, Friedrich Wilhelm Ludolf Gerhard Augustin von Steuben, is a bit of a mouthful, and we now know him simply as Baron Von Steuben. His birth to Royal Prussian Engineer, Capt. Baron Wilhelm von Steuben and Elizabeth von Jagvodin took place in the Prussian military fortress town of Magdeburg, Germany.

Military Training

He trained from early manhood as a soldier, first serving with his father as a volunteer in the War of the Austrian Succession at age fourteen. In 1747 he joined the Prussian Army and served in the Seven Years War, getting wounded at the Battle of Prague. He received another wound at the Battle of Kunersdorf in 1759 during the same war. The Russians took him prisoner at Major General von Knoblock's surrender on the eastern front. *In* 1762, the Russians released him, when he received a promotion to captain. This promotion eventually led to his appointment as aide-de-camp to Frederick the Great.

Traveling Soldier

When the war ended in 1763, the Army reduced its forces and released Von Steuben. He found employment serving as Grand Marshall for Fürst Josef Friedrich Wilhelm of Hohenzollern-Hechingen from 1764 until 1777. It was during this time he became acquainted with French Minister of War

(Count de St. Germaine). During 1771 the Prince of Hollenzollern-Hechingen bestowed the title "Baron" to him, thus he now became Baron Von Steuben.

Meeting Benjamin Franklin

He was looking for work as a soldier in 1777 when he traveled to France in 1777. French Foreign Minister Comte de Saint-Germaine sensed the value that a former Prussian Army officer could have to the American cause. By now allied to America, St. Germaine introduced him to Benjamin Franklin, who in turn recommended him to General George Washington via letter. Washington wrote back that the Continental Congress could promise neither pay nor rank and he would have to present himself to Congress as a volunteer.

Refusal To Serve as Volunteer in American Cause

Disgusted, he returned to Prussia to find allegations of improper relationships while in Prince Josef Friedrich Wilhelm of Hohenzollern-Hechingen's service. The allegations carried charges of homosexual conduct, never proven, and would prove disastrous for his hopes of military promotion.

Acceptance

He returned to Paris and accepted Franklin's proposal. The French government paid his passage, and he arrived in Philadelphia in December 1, 1777. Because he had outfitted himself in a red uniform, the Americans mistook him for a British officer and almost arrested him. After Congress reviewed him and made arrangements for payment at the conclusion of the war, the Congress sent him to General Washington. General Washington received him on February 23, 1778.

Inspector General

The General appointed Von Steuben Inspector General with the task of write standard drills for an army that used different training methods from company to company. Since he could not write English, he wrote his orders in the military language of Europe, French. Washington's aides-de-camps, John Laurens and Alexander Hamilton, translated the orders into English. Brigade inspectors then copied the lessons into the orderly book for each brigade and regiment. He also instituted a change in the layout of the camps. Before his arrival the soldiers relieved themselves anywhere they wished. They killed animals for consumption in the middle of the camp and left the remains in place. He reorganized the entire camp, placing the latrines on the lower end and the kitchens on the upper end of the camp.

Military Training Program

Using the skills he learned in the best military in the world, the Prussian Army, he upgraded the training drills practiced by the soldiers under Washington's command. He hand picked 120 soldiers and used them as incubators for his training methods. Because he used profanity in several languages profusely and worked directly with the soldiers, they loved him and with eagerness learned his methods. They, in turn, went out and trained the other soldiers.

Training the Continental Army

His training transformed the Continental Army, which became evident at their first battle, the Battle of Stony Point, fought on July 16, 1779. The Americans won that engagement. During the years of 1778 through 1779 the Baron developed his *Regulations for the Order and Discipline of the Troops of the United States,* This book was commonly known as the "Blue Book" and the army used it until 1814, though its practices influenced the Army until the Mexican War of 1846.

American Citizen

After a stint with illness, he rejoined the army on April 27, 1779. He served at the Yorktown campaign. After the war, he helped Washington demobilize the army. The Army discharged him "With Honor" in 1784 and in March 1784 the Pennsylvania legislature granted him American citizenship.

The Congress, due to lack of funds, could never pay him what it promised. New York, Pennsylvania, and Virginia each granted him lands. He sold portions of these lands, finally retiring to some holdings in New York, where he died in 1794.

Henry Knox (July 25, 1750 – October 25, 1806)

The son of William and Mary Campbell Knox, Henry was a native of Boston. He attended the Boston Latin School until his father died when he was twelve years old. Henry quit school to support his mother, taking a job at a bookstore. Knox joined the Siege of Boston in 1775 and, at General George Washington's direction, traveled to Fort Ticonderoga to retrieve cannon from that British fort after it fell to the Americans. He engineered a successful campaign to bring the cannon and other supplies to Boston to help push the British out of that vital port. He participated in several campaigns during the Revolutionary War. After the war Congress appointed him as the second Secretary of War, a position he held until 1794.

March 1793 - Fort St. Clair Constructed

Colonel James Wilkinson decided that the distance between Fort Jefferson and Fort Hamilton was too great, so he had his troops and the militias under his command construct the fort in March, 1792. The walls were 120 foot long and the stockade had a bastion at each corner. The fort stood near a spring that fed into Seven Mile Creek, to which it was adjacent. The fort's site is now inside Fort St. Clair State Park on the southwestern edge of Eaton, Ohio, near the Indiana/Ohio State line. At the time of its construction each Fort St. Clair's garrison consisted of 129 soldiers commanded by seven officers. Fort Hamilton had 105 soldiers and two officers. Fort Washington's garrison consisted of 77 soldiers and nine officers.

Fort St. Clair State Park

395 Camden Road

Eaton OH 45320

March 14, 1792 - John Francis Hamtramck Negotiates Treaty with Natives

Several small groups of tribes from the Eel River in addition to a few contingents of the Wea tribe negotiated a treaty with General John Hamtramck at Vincennes. The treaty signing took place on March 14, 1792. The treaty contained a provision that the tribes would assist in bringing the Kickapoo tribe into negotiating peace with the United States. If the Kickapoo refused to participate, the tribes that signed the treaty must help expel them from the region.

March 30, 1792 - St. Clair Requests Court Martial

Many in Congress and around the nation called for an investigation into St. Clair's conduct during the disastrous campaign. St. Clair offered to tender his officer's commission and requested a court martial, which he felt would clear his name.

April 1792

April 03, 1792 - Major Alexander Trueman Receives Instructions from Knox

In an attempt to make peace with the Wabash Indian tribes, Secretary of War Henry Knox instructed Major Alexander Trueman to travel to Kekionga and deliver a message of peace to the tribes assembled there. He was to attempt to aid a mission he was giving to Rufus Putnam and convince the tribes to visit Philadelphia to conduct treaty negotiations. The United States had recently conducted peace missions with several of the tribes in the southern United States, including the Creeks, Cherokees, Chickasaws, and Choctaws. He was to show them the treaties signed with these nations to convince them to join the Iroquois tribes then meeting in Philadelphia. Knox instructed Trueman to depart on the mission as soon as possible.

Alexander Trueman (1755 - 1792)

The son of Henry and Ann Magruder Truman, Alexander was native to Maryland. He and Margaret Reynolds married and had three children.

Truman had received promotion from lieutenant to Major in April 1792.

April 07, 1792 - St. Clair Resigns Commission

General Arthur St. Clair tendered his resignation from his commission and from the Army. He continued to serve as governor of the Northwest Territory.

April 07, 1792 - Wilkinson Dispatches Two Peace Missions

Lieutenant Colonel James Wilkinson dispatches two parties of men headed by Major Alexander Trueman and Isaac Freeman charged with delivering letters of peace to the Indians along the Wabash.

The Parties

Major Alexander Trueman and John Hardin made up one of the parties. Isaac Freeman and Joseph Gerrard made up the other. Others in the small peace delegation included William Smalley, Thomas Flinn. Flinn, Gerrard and Smalley served as interpreters. A soldier, William Lynch, also accompanied the party to serve as a waiter to Trueman. Trueman took a small pony to serve as a pack animal for his supplies. The two parties departed from Columbia, now the neighborhood of Columbia-Tusculum on the east side of Cincinnati, on April 7, 1792. The men entered Harmar's Trace and began their journey.

John Hardin (Oct 1, 1753 - circa May 1792)

The son of Martin Hardin and Lydia Waters, John was native to Elk Run, Virginia. The family moved to George's Creek, Pennsylvania in 1765. Growing up on the frontier provided Hardin with an education in the ways of the woods, and he became an expert in the art of woodcraft. He put those skills to use in the 1774 Lord Dunmore's War and later with Daniel Morgan's Rifle Corps during the Revolutionary War. Hardin saw plenty of action during the Northwest Indian Wars in the Northwest Territory. In the future state of Indiana Hardin led strikes against the natives near Vincennes in 1786 and to Terre Haute in 1789.

Battle of Heller's Corner

Harmar sent Hardin out on October 15 with about 200 men to scout the area. This force consisted of about 30 United States regular troops and about 170 militiamen. A single warrior appeared in front of the force, which the soldiers began to pursue. Lured by the decoy, Hardin's troops rode into an ambush in swampy lowlands near the Eel River. The natives killed twenty-two of the regulars and forty militiamen. Some refer to the battle as Hardin's Defeat. Many credit Miami Chief Little Turtle with leading the attack, however there is conflicting evidence that he did.

Speech

Hardin, on special mission from Wilkinson, carried letters containing speeches written by President George Washington. He had addressed the speeches to the "Wyandottes, Chippewas, Pottawattamies, and all other tribes residing southward of the lakes, east of the Mississippi, and northward of the Ohio River." In the letter, Washington tried to convince the sachems and warriors of these tribes that they should forsake war and take up a life of agriculture. He offered to give them the things they needed to do this and to teach them how to cultivate the earth, raise oxen and other domestic animals, build comfortable houses, educate their children and forever inhabit their lands. He implored them to attend a peace conference at Philadelphia in which they would not have to give up any more lands. He promised that the United States would take care of the chiefs that attended and that they would conduct them safely to and from the conference and feed them while they attended. Isaac Freeman carried a similar letter.

Departure

The two parties departed together and would travel along Harmar's Trace for several days before separating to accomplish their separate missions.

April 13, 1792 - Anthony Wayne Appointed Commander of the Legion of the United States

On April 13, 1792, George Washington appointed Anthony Wayne as commander of the Legion of the United States.

Anthony Wayne (January 1, 1745 – December 15, 1796)

One of five children born to Isaac Wayne and Elizabeth Iddings Wayne, Anthony was a native of Paoli Pennsylvania. He trained as a surveyor at his uncle's private Philadelphia academy and at the College of Philadelphia. He did not earn a degree despite being first in his class. He went to Nova Scotia to survey some of property there, spending about a year there. After finishing that project, he went to work at his father's tannery business while doing survey work on the side. He married Mary Penrose in 1766, with whom he had two children.

Military and the Revolutionary War

The unfortunate nickname "Mad" became attached to Anthony, probably because of his temper. The nickname ignores the fact that Anthony Wayne was an excellent officer that believed strongly in good planning, training and execution of his plans. He became a colonel of the 4th Pennsylvania Regiment and learned about discipline, training and preparation during the time he was stationed at Fort Ticonderoga. He fought at the Battle of Germantown, Monmouth and at Monmouth Courthouse. He rose in rank steadily becoming a brigadier general in 1777. He was with General George Washington at Valley Forge and Washington learned to rely on his military skills during that difficult time and in several battles afterwards.

Politics

After the war ended, Wayne served one year in the Pennsylvania Legislature. After this, he moved to Georgia and attended the convention that ratified the United States

Constitution. The voters of Georgia elected him to the United States House of Representatives in 1791; however, he lost the seat in a residency dispute. He declined to run again.

April 15, 1792 - Trueman and Freeman Parties Separate

On or about April 15, 1792 Trueman, Freeman and the others paused to hold a meeting about mid-afternoon. Freeman and Trueman's missions took them different directions. Freeman was to proceed to the Indian town of Sandusky and Trueman towards Kekionga. Isaac Freeman, John Gerrard, and John Hardin turned northeast, while Trueman, Smalley and William Lynch the northwest.

Isaac Freeman (1768 - 1792)

One of the early settlers of Cincinnati, Freeman purchased a lot on January 7, 1789, when he and a man named Jonas Menser purchased tracts that lay between Front, Second, Sycamore and Broadway ; Second, Third, Sycamore and Broadway; Front, Second, Sycamore and Main and the east half of the block bounded by Second, Third, Sycamore and Main streets. Freeman had volunteered for at least one peace mission before, in 1789.

Freeman's First Mission

In mid-June 1789, Freeman had volunteered for a dangerous mission into Indian country to undertake a mission to exchange some prisoners as the whites held several Indians and the Indians had taken many whites prisoner. John Cleves Symmes had proposed the meeting, for which a number of men volunteered. He selected Freeman for the mission, from which he did not expect the young man to return. Symmes felt that if the did survive to return, he would later serve as an invaluable guide, as few white men had visited the territory that Freeman would traverse during his mission. He also selected a fifteen-year-old Shawnee boy that had been held prisoner in Kentucky as an interpreter. The party departed sometime in mid to late June carrying twenty days provisions on one packhorse. Symmes had spurred the settlers to begin building a stockade as a defense against further Indian attacks in case Freeman's mission failed.

Lodging with Blue Jacket

Freeman arrived at the Shawnee village where Blue Jacket made his home, somewhere along the Maumee River. He lodged with Blue Jacket and gave him the message written by Symmes. Blue Jacket agreed to the prisoner exchange and had a reply to Symmes drafted. Freeman returned on July 17, 1789 with four prisoners.

Freeman's Report

Freeman reported that the Indians of the Maumee and Wabash River regions were well along with their preparations for war. They intended to destroy the settlements along the Miami River. They only waited for the supplies needed for them to do so. During his short stay in the Shawnee town, he saw pack horses bringing ample supplies of gunpowder and lead shot delivered from the British post at Detroit. He also saw numerous British flags displayed around the village. In the same shipment, he noted the delivery of one hundred muskets. He observed several stores of weapons, powder and shot stored in numerous places around the village.

April 16 - 1792 - Isaac Freeman, John Gerard, and John Hardin Killed

Author Note: The next several dates are approximate, having been reconstructed from Smalley's account. His account was not written by him, but related by an acquaintance or family member after his death in 1838. The

account is recorded in the Indiana Historical Society Publications, Volume 1 by the Indiana Historical Society.

On, or about, April 16, 1792, a band of Indians encountered the Freeman party sometime after they separated from the Truman party. One of the Indians in the group later related, possibly to John Smalley as he was held prisoner, that they had killed all three. They tomahawked Joseph Gerard and shot Hardin. Isaac Freeman fled when he saw what was happening. One of the Indians shot him, hitting him in the arm and breaking it. They then chased him down and tomahawked him.

April 15, 1792 - Trueman and Lynch Killed

Meeting Indians on the Trail

Trueman, Lynch and Smalley traveled along the Trace, carrying a white flag of truce, until they reached a point somewhere along the Auglaize River, southeast of Kekionga. Here, they met three Indians, one of whom was a boy of about fourteen and the other an old man. The boy was the son of the third Indian, a younger man.

Smalley, the interpreter, hailed them, saying, "We are on an errand of peace, the white people want to have peace and have sent this man, (indicating Major Trueman), to make proposals for peace."

Camping

Smalley proposed that the men camp together.

The Indians agreed, after a brief consultation. Trueman directed Lynch to prepare some chocolate, after which Trueman requested that the Indians dine with them on the chocolate. While they supped, Smalley, as the only one that spoke the language, attempted to convince the Indians that it would be to their advantage to trade their furs with the

Americans rather than the British at Detroit. He related that the Americans would trade the Indian's meat for powder and shot. The warriors appeared pleased with the proposal.

Deception

Trueman, who had a severe cold, said that he would lie down. He spread some bearskins on the ground, lay down and covered himself with a blanket. The young Indian man requested of Smalley that he tie one of the men because the white party was stronger than the Indian one, which consisted of the boy, old man and the boy's father. The boy, he said, was afraid to go to sleep. Trueman allowed the father to tie Lynch. The Indian stripped the bark off a tree and tied Lynch, but did not tie him very tight. Smalley also made his bed and lay down, however he propped himself up and continued conversing with the older Indian. They talked about the previous year's hunting season. The old Indian remarked that he had had poor luck, partly because of the condition of his gun. As the Indian showed Smalley his gun, Trueman had a severe coughing spell during which the Indian shot him, killing him instantly.

Death of Lynch

Upon hearing the shot, Smalley leapt to his feet and fled into the forest. The other Indian fired at him, but missed. The Indian boy ran off, also. Lynch began struggling to free himself. The younger Indian, afraid that Lynch would succeed in freeing himself, struck the man in the head with a tomahawk several times. Lynch, severely wounded, was not dead.

Smalley's Dilemma

Almost paralyzed by fear, Smalley stayed hidden in the forest. He considered running, but dismissed the idea, as he was eight days from Fort Washington and had only a butcher knife on him. The Indians tried to convince him to return to the fire, but Smalley demurred, saying that they would kill him as they had killed the others. The Indian said that he had wanted Trueman's gun and that they would not kill Smalley. The Indian persisted, and Smalley, realizing that they had not reloaded their guns, agreed to return to the fire if they would place their guns, tomahawks and knives out of reach, which they did. Smalley concealed his butcher knife and returned to the fire.

Captive

As he sat down, the boy returned. The old Indian directed the boy to kill Lynch, as he was growing tired of his groaning. The boy did and then scalped him, again at the direction of the old man. The old Indian told Smalley to dress the scalp, which revolted the man, but he did it. Smalley considered pulling his knife and killing one of the Indians. He figured that with the element of surprise he could kill one, but not both. Afraid that killing one would lead to his immediate death, he refrained. The Indians eventually convinced him that they would not kill him, but would take him to see their king the next day. Smalley spent the rest of the gloomy night considering his fate. During their conversations, Smalley related to the natives that he had been captured as a boy. He had lived among the Indians for many years. He told them that he had gone on the mission with the others because he had wanted to return to his former life among the Indians.

April 17, 1792 - William Smalley Before King Boconjehaulis

On the morning after his capture by the Indians, they took him to the town of a chief they called King Boconjehaulis for questioning. Smalley repeated the story that he had told the evening before, that he had been held captives by Indians as a boy and that if they could bring his Indian father, that he would confirm his story. Smalley told them the conditions of his release and that the tribe he dwelt with had said he could return someday, if that was his wish. He also said that he had grown tired of life among the whites and that he had gone on the mission in hopes of returning to that life. He did not mention his white wife and children and that he was desperately worried about them and wanted to return to allay their fears over his disappearance.

One Indian present during the questioning professed to know the Indian Smalley claimed was his father and would be willing to go after him, as it was only about a two or three day journey to the village. Boconjehaulis consented, however, the questioning continued sporadically for the remainder of the day.

William Smalley (c.1762 - September 30 1838)

The son of Benjamin Smalley Jr. and Rachel Cresson Smalley, William was probably native to Cumberland, New Jersey. Sometime around 1764 the family moved to the region around Fort Pitt in Western Pennsylvania. Sometime around 1768 he and several other settlers stood guard around the fields to warn of Indian attack while the other settlers planted crops. In spite of their watchfulness, a band of Delaware Indians crept between the settlers and the fort and attacked them. During the conflict, they captured the survivors and William watched as a warrior tomahawked his father to death. He witnessed the butcher of most of the other people, after which they took him and a few others to their village along the Maumee River.

Prisoner

The Indians confined the prisoners to a hut they kept for holding captives. They forced William to run the gauntlet while they beat him with sticks, clubs and rocks. William survived the ordeal. They bored holes in his ears and cut them until they hung in strips. During his captivity he watched the American survivors of the June 5, 1782 Battle of Sandusky, including Colonel William Crawford, tortured to death. Other atrocities he witnessed while held included seeing a white woman's baby ripped from her breast and thrown into a fire. He learned the native tongue as well as French during the years of his captivity.

Escape

Sometime around 1784 the Delaware authorized him to lead a peace mission to the French in Louisiana to regain the French market for their furs. They promised him that they would free him if his succeeded in the mission. He did complete it and they released him. He returned to the Fort Pitt area where he married Prudence Hoel. The couple would have ten children.

Guide and Soldier

Sometime around 1788 he moved his family to Columbia, which was near Fort Washington. He served as a guide and hunter for surveying parties in the region, receiving seventy-five cents a day for his services. He served during and survived both Harmar's Defeat and St. Clair's defeat. Historical lore indicates he discharged his weapon thirty-five times during the battle, hitting his mark twenty times.

Guide for Isaac Truman Expedition

His experience and knowledge of the native languages made him a natural choice for the 1792 peace expedition.

April 18, 1792 - Joseph Gerard's Head Brought into Camp

On Smalley's second day of captivity, he witnessed the head of a white man elevated on a pole brought into camp. He was certain that the head looked like that of Joseph Gerard, a member of the other peace mission.

Joseph Gerard (1763 - 1792)

The son of Elias and Rachel Gerard, Joseph was native to Fort Cumberland, Maryland. He married Elizabeth Crist, with whom he had four children. Gerard had migrated into the Fort Washington area with his family. He had volunteered to go with Hardin's mission. He had been promised substantial financial reward if the mission was successful.

May 1792

Early May - 1792 - Smalley Reunited With His Indian Father

About two weeks after Smalley's capture his Indian father and brother came to camp in company with the Indian that had gone looking for them. During this interval, Boconjehaulis questioned Smalley every day in hopes of catching him in a contradiction. The Indians confirmed Smalley's story and took him back to their village.

Fear of Exposure

Smalley considered escape; however, he knew that if he did, his Indian father would die at the hands of the others. During his stay at his Indian father's village, the Indians brought in an acquaintance of Smalley's as a prisoner. Smalley feared the man would mention Smalley's wife and children, exposing his concealment of this fact. If the Indians found out he had a wife and children they would know Smalley had lied about wanting to live with them again and kill him. He did tell his adopted father about his family and that he wanted to return.

Escape Plan

The Indian said he would do what he could to allow him to do so, but they would have to be careful. He said that they would plan a hunting trip and that Smalley could escape during it and his Indian father could say that Smalley escaped in the night and that the Indians could not catch up to him. The plan settled on, Smalley waited, in fear of exposure and death each day.

May 05, 1792 - Rufus Putnam Appointed Brigadier General

On May 5, 1792 President George Washington appointed Rufus Putnam as brigadier general.

Rufus Putnam (April 9, 1738 – May 4, 1824)

The son of Elisha and Susan Fuller Putnam, Rufus was native to Sutton, Massachusetts. His father died when he was seven and his mother sent him to live temporarily with her father in Danvers, Massachusetts. During the time he lived with his grandfather he attended school and learned to read the Bible. His mother married an innkeeper, John Sadler, in 1747.

Education

His stepfather, illiterate himself, mocked Rufus' attempt to continue his education and did not send him to school. Rufus improved his reading, writing and arithmetic studies in spite of his stepfather's scorn. In 1754 millwright John Sadler took him on as an apprentice. Millwright also did not encourage Putnam's attempts educate himself, however he did allow the boy to have a lamp in the evening with which to study. Putnam focused his studies on arithmetic, geography, surveying and history. Putnam lamented his poor spelling and writing skills his entire life.

French and Indian War

On March 15, 1757 Putnam enlisted in the militia to fight in the French and Indian War. He joined Captain Been Learned's company, which traveled to the Great Lakes region for extensive service. He served under Captain Israel Putnam, which was part of the garrison of Fort Edward, which is on the Hudson River. Putnam was assigned to serve a scout for Lieutenant Colonel Joseph Frye's infantry regiment during a six day mission to South Bay on July 8. During this mission his commander sent Putnam and two other men on a scouting trip to the bay. The men, desiring to travel light and believing that their destination was not far, left their blankets and provisions. It had been further than they expected and they did not return until sunset and the company's commander had become frightened and ordered the company to leave their camp. Putnam's company returned to camp to find it deserted. They attempted t to track the company without success and spent two nights without provisions or blankets, afflicted by hunger, gnats and mosquitoes. The fired their muskets in an attempt to signal the company to no avail. Tired, hungry and mosquito bitten, the men returned to Fort Edward on July 11. His commander, thinking they were dead or taken by Indians, reported this to the Lieutenant Colonel Putnam and was surprised at their return. During one action a few days later he witnessed the savagery of an Indian attack, a sight which left an impression on the young soldier.

Eating Dog

He took part in Lieutenant Colonel Israel Putnam's, who was a cousin to him, retaliatory attack. The colonel's attention to detail and leadership impressed Putnam of the importance of both during this campaign. During another march in February 1758 his company, bereft of provisions while on a long winter trek, was forced to eat the dog that accompanied them on the mission. He reported that dog meat was tasty and that he would eat it again if circumstances warranted it.

Reenlistment

He returned home when his term expired, however he enlisted again on April 10, 1758, serving in the company of Captain Joseph Whitcomb under the command of Colonel Timothy Ruggle. He returned home on December 6 and resolved to not enlist again. However in March 1760 he again enlisted, answering a call for another campaign. He served most of this term at Fort Ticonderoga, where he saw little action. He returned to his home in New Brantree Massachusetts, where he took up his trade as a millwright.

Civilian Life

He married Elizabeth Ayres, who died in 1762, probably while delivering their son. He married Persis Rice on January 25, 1765, with whom he would have ten children. During the next several years he worked as a millwright, studying and learning the surveying trade. In 1769 he became a surveyor and took up farming. 1773 he and Israel Putnam traveled to Pensacola, Florida, where they would survey land along the Mississippi River that the British government wanted to grant to soldiers that served in the French and Indian War as payment.

Surveying in Florida

He departed New Brantree on December 10, 1772 and arrived at Israel Putnam's home in Brooklyn, Connecticut on December 11. The men boarded the Mississippi, a sloop owned by Military Company of Adventurers, on January 10, 1773. Seasickness plagued Putnam the entire journey until they landed at Môle-Saint-Nicolas, which is a port on the northeastern coast of Haiti January 30. They stayed on Haiti until February 4, when they departed for Jamaica, coming ashore in Montenegro Bay. The Putnam cousins left Montenegro Bay on February 8. They passed the west end of Cuba and endured a violent squall, finally making port at Pensacola on March 1. The departed Pensacola on 18 and reached the Mississippi River's mouth on March 22. The passed New Orleans and sailed upstream until April 8, when the captain would not allow the sloop to travel any further upstream. They climbed aboard a bateaux and began exploring, traveling as far north as the Big Black River's mouth in the Mississippi, about twenty five miles south of present day Vicksburg. They traveled upstream about twenty-five miles, finding valuable land as they went.

Black River

However, an Indian chief informed them that he would allow them to settle along the mouth of the Black River and no further. Thus, the Putnam cousins returned to the mouth of the river and spent several days exploring and mapping out several townships. Their work complete, they returned to Pensacola on July 5 to lay out their report to the Royal Governor of West Florida. They tried unsuccessfully to have the governor grant them additional time to work on the settlement, to no avail. Thus, they departed Pensacola on July 12 and returned to New London, Connecticut on August 10. The Putnam cousin's work came to naught, as the development was delayed, then halted due to hostilities erupting between Britain and her colonies in April, 1775.

Revolutionary War

Putnam volunteered and enlisted, receiving the rank of lieutenant colonel serving in Colonel David Brewer. He fought at the Battle of Bunker Hill and shortly thereafter received appointment as Engineer of Defensive Works on June 17, 1775.

May 08, 1792 - Henry Knox Requests Hendrick Aupaumut Undertake Peace Mission

Secretary of War Henry Knox, attempting to avoid war with the western native tribes, requested that Hendrick Aupaumut travel to the Lake Erie region carrying messages of peace to the Great Council of Indians at Lake Erie. During their meeting, Aupaumut received an allotment of silver ear and nose jewels to present the natives.

Hendrick Aupaumut (1757-1830)

Probably descended from Mohawk chief Hendrick, Hendrick was native to Stockbridge, Massachusetts and a member of the Stockbridge-Mohican tribe. Moravian missionaries provided his education. Hendrick joined the Continental Army when the Revolutionary War on June 23, 1775.

Revolutionary War Service

Aupaumut joined the Continental Army as a private, joining Captain William Goodrich's Company of Indians. The company formed a part of Colonel John Patterson's Regiment. Aupaumut's company helped Benedict Arnold's forces during their retreat from Canada in 1776. This unit served during the Siege of Boston and as a scout during serving under Captains Nimham during the Saratoga campaign in 1777. When his captain died during the massacre of Stockbridge Indians in the Bronx, New York he assumed command of his company. He was one of the survivors of the massacre. George Washington promoted him to captain in 1779. Aupaumut remained in the service of the Continental Army until 1782.

After the War

Aupaumut became friends with the Mohegan minister, Samson Occum and supported him in his ministry. General George Washington presented him with a sword in 1791 in appreciation for his service. He accompanied his tribe when they moved from their town in Stockbridge, Massachusetts to Oneida Creek, New York, where they founded New Stockbridge. Northwest Territory Governor Arthur asked him to carry a message of peace to the Northwest tribes in 1791.

Stockbridge-Mohican Tribe

Calling themselves the "Muh-he-con-neok" ("People of the Waters that are Never Still,") the Stockbridge Indians were a mix of tribes that consisted of elements of the Mahican, Housatonic, Wappinger, Tunxis, Shawnee and other tribes that had formerly inhabited the Hudson River area. These native peoples assembled at Stockbridge in the middle 1750's to form a "Praying Town," of natives that had converted to Christianity and adopted white ways, while preserving some elements of their own culture. A number of these praying towns had formed in New England and New York as the Indians tried to navigate the delicate balance of the pressures that the expanding white population placed on their lands, culture and population. In spite of the fact that the Stockbridge Indians had sided with the British during the French and Indian War and had fought during Pontiac's Rebellion, the Americans inflicted injustices upon the tribe.

Post French/Indian War

After the French and Indian War, the colonists excluded the natives from their town councils, used their courts against them and spied on their movements. Squatters stole their land and used other methods to steal their land. At the time of the Revolution, the Stockbridge Indians had allowed Moravian missionaries to live among them and they had, in spite of the injustices inflicted upon them, supported the American cause during the Revolution. The Indians perhaps saw a way to preserve what remained of their lands and culture if they supported the Americans. Additionally, their community was surrounded on all sides by whites, so not to support them was an invitation for the whites to attack them. When the fighting broke out in April 1775, many of the men had joined with the minutemen in firing on the British as they retreated from Concord and Lexington. The Company of Indians had formed in early May 1775, with many of the men joining the company formed by Captain William Goodrich.

May 10, 1792 - Hendrick Aupaumut Departs Philadelphia

Hendrick Aupaumut departed Philadelphia on May 10 for his mission to carry messages of peace to the Northwest Tribes. He and his younger brother traveled 190 northwest miles in seven days, arriving at Tioga Point, Pennsylvania, near the New York Border on May 17. Once there, he discovered that the chiefs of the Seneca, Onagonda and Cayuga had departed, bound for Canandaigua. Aupaumut sent his brother to Oneida, New York, a distance of about 90 miles to fetch his peace bag and a strand of ancient wampum to bring them to council with the native chiefs. To further impress upon them of the importance of his message, he asked his brother to gather his best counselors and to meet him at Canandaigua. Aupaumut departed on the seventy mile journey to Canandaigua.

May 18, 1792 - John Heckeweller Receives Letter Requesting Aid in Crafting Treaty

On May 18, 1792, Moravian missionary John Heckeweller received a letter from Secretary of War Henry Knox requesting his help in making peace with the Wabash tribes. In the letter, Knox requests that Heckeweller accompany General Rufus Putnam, who the Secretary had given authority to conclude a treaty with the Indian tribes, to assist him. Heckeweller presented the letter to the Moravian Elders in Bethlehem and received their blessing to undertake the endeavor.

John Heckeweller (March 12, 1743 - January 31, 1823)

The son of David and Christine "Rosina" Heckewelder, John was native to Bedford, England. His parents, Moravian missionaries of German descent, had earlier migrated from Germany to flee religious persecution. On March 12, 1754 the Heckeweller family departed England on the ship Irene, bound for New York. After a quick passage of only twenty-one days, the family stayed with some Moravian families living in the city. John, accompanied by David Nitschmann, traveled by foot from New York to Bethlehem, Pennsylvania, which at the time was the center of the Moravian church in the United States. Since there were no bridges across most of the streams on their route, Nitschmann carried the eleven year old boy across them.

Education and Apprenticeship

Heckeweller had attended Moravian schools while in England and in Bethlehem attended another Moravian school in company with the older boys. After two years he went to Christiansburg to work as a field hand and perform other manual labor. In 1758 cedar cooper William Nixon took him on as an apprentice. Heckeweller performed his duties; however his dream was to become a Moravian missionary working among the Indians to convert them to Christianity.

T rip to Northwest Territory

Moravian missionary David Post had traveled into the Northwest Territory three times doing missionary work among the Indian tribes. In 1762 he decided to make another journey. He chose Heckeweller as a companion on the mission.

Beginning the Journey

The men departed Bethlehem on March 8, passed through Lancaster and reached the Susquehanna River. Spring snowmelt had caused the river to rise, creating a raging current. The ferryman at first refused to cross the river due to the treacherous waters. Post prevailed upon them and he finally relented. The current carried the ferry almost a mile downstream before they reached safety on the other side.

They passed through Carlisle, where they stopped to confer with other Moravians, and then continued to Sharpsburg, which was the last of the intact white settlements. After reaching this village, the only towns they passed were fire blackened ruins, testament to the ferocity of the French and Indian War, which would not end for another year. By March 30, they reached the Appalachian Mountains. As they began ascending the mountains, snow began to fall. It reached a depth of about three feet, slowing the travelers and creating a painful trek.

Site of Massacre

Upon approaching Fort Pitt, the men unexpectedly came upon the site of Braddock's Defeat, which had occurred on July 12, 1755. The sight of human bones scattered over the ground horrified them as they passed through the battlefield.

At Fort Pitt

At Fort Pitt, they had expected to purchase flour and other provisions, however the Indians had laid siege to the fort, cutting off supplies. The men dined on horsemeat and departed the fort, crossing the Allegheny River on April 5.

Failure

After the crossing they spent a wet night as they attempted to keep their supplies dry during a heavy thunderstorm. After many hardships crossing rain swollen streams, they reached their destination, a Tuscorora village in which they entered a cabin the Indians had allowed Post to build in the village on April 11. The negotiations eventually failed. Post had left Heckeweller at the village, continuing his mission to the Indians further west. The Indians warned Heckeweller that he should leave, relations had deteriorated. Heckeweller, sick with fever and weak from the poor diet, left the village in company with a trader, a Mr. Calhoun. The men reached Pittsburg on the third week in October. He returned to Bethlehem a few days later.

Partnership with David Zeisburger

After the failed mission, Heckeweller worked with the various Moravian missions in Pennsylvania. In 1771 David Zeisburger traveled to Bethlehem and requested that Heckeweller join him in his quest to found Moravian missions on the frontier. The men founded the first settlement in Ohio, Schoenbrunn, in 1772, and the first school in 1773.

Schoenbrunn Village

The Delaware Indian chief Netawatwes invited Zeisberger to found a village in along the Tuscarawas River in the Ohio Country in 1772. Zeisberger and several Delaware families moved into the area, found a suitable site and founded their village. The villagers built cabins and planted gardens that included corn, beans, squash, potatoes and turnips. The built the first school house in Ohio and established the first civil code. The council consisted of Zeisberger, several Moravians and Delaware converts. The Delaware established the rules for the settlement. The village prospered for several years; however the tensions created by the Revolutionary War proved too great and by 1777 the villagers abandoned the settlement. Schoenbrunn Village has been restored. Those interested in visiting the restored village may contact:

Schoenbrunn Village

1984 E. High Avenue

New Philadelphia, OH 44663

800.752.2711

https://www.ohiohistory.org/visit/museum-and-site-locator/schoenbrunn-village

May 25, 1792 - Hendrick Aupaumut Meets with Joseph Brandt

By May 25, 1792 Hendrick Aupaumut had arrived in Canandaigua where he met up with his brother and the men he had sent for. At the settlement he waited for General Israel Chapin, the general that would head up the negotiations, who was busy meeting with leaders of the Five Nations. While he waited he met with Mohawk Chief Joseph Brandt.

Canandaigua

Located in northwestern New York halfway between Buffalo, to the west, and Syracuse to the east, Canandaigua grew up near site of an important Seneca town called Onnaghee, Onaghee or Onahie. American settlers made the first permanent dwellings in the town they would first call Ga-nun-da-gwa, and then later Canandaigua in 1789. By the time Aupaumut arrived, the town already had several buildings and had been connected by a road to Utica. The Seneca town still existed nearby.

Joseph Brant (March 1742/3 - November 24, 1807)

The son of Peter and Margaret Tehonwaghkwangearahkwa, Joseph was born near the Muskingum River in the present state of Ohio during a hunting trip. His Mohawk name, Thayendanegea, means "he who places two bets" or ""two sticks bound together for strength". His father died shortly after Joseph's birth, so his mother returned to their home in Canajoharie, New York.

Education

His mother, a successful businesswoman who dealt in ginseng, married a Mohawk Chief named Brant, also successful in business. Kanagradunckwa was a close friend of British Indian agent William Johnson, who stayed with the family when he was staying along the Mohawk River. He took an interest in Joseph's sister Mary, also called Molly. The two began living together and Joseph decided he wanted to live with them. Johnson helped provide Brandt with an education, which was interrupted by the outbreak of the Seven Years War (French and Indian War.)

French and Indian War

During this conflict Brandt participated in several British campaigns in Canada, notably the Battle of Fort Niagara, the Battle of Fort Carillon and along the St. Lawrence River. His actions earned him a silver medal. During the Montreal campaign, the British captured Fort Lévis. British General Jeffery Amherst refused to allow the warriors to enter the fort as he feared they would massacre the French soldiers for their scalps. The Mohawks returned to their homes; however Brandt remained to aid the British in their campaign to take Montreal.

Further Education

In 1761 Johnson arranged for Brandt to attend With Johnson and Brandt's assistance, Joseph attended Eleazar Wheelock's Moor's Charity School for Indians in Lebanon, Connecticut. Wheelock took charge of Brandt's education, teaching him English, as well as other topics. The outbreak of Pontiac's (French and Indian) interrupted Joseph's education.

Pontiac's Rebellion

Brandt had left school for a short period and had planned to continue his education by attending King's College in New York City; however the outbreak of hostilities between the natives and whites created a hostile environment for the Indians, so Brandt did not go. Instead, he joined Johnson's efforts to quell the rebellion and restore peace. In 1764

Brandt led a war party into the Susquehanna and Chemung valleys to attack Delaware villages in the area. Since he spoke English and a number of the Iroquois languages, the British Indian Department hired him as an interpreter in 1766.

Marriage and Settling Down

On July 22, 1765 Brandt married Peggie, with whom he had two children. Peggy was a white woman, reportedly taken captive by the Indians while a young girl in Virginia. The couple lived in the home his stepfather had bequeathed him when he died. Additionally, Brandt had an 80 acre farm which he worked in addition to tending a small store.

Before the War

Johnson and Peggy lived in the house until she died of tuberculosis in 1771, leaving him with two children to care for. The next year he moved to Fort Hunter, near Florida, New York, to act as an interpreter and teacher for Reverend John Stuart. Brandt had received appointment as an official in the British Indian Department in early 1775. Additionally, Johnson had encouraged the Mohawk to make Brandt a war chief at the end of the French and Indian War, thus he had influence with both the British and the Mohawk.

Travel to London

William Johnson Takes Mohawk Chief Joseph Brandt to England

When hostilities between the colonists and the British broke out in April 1775, both the Americans and the British courted the Iroquois nations at the start of the conflict. To induce the Mohawks to join with the British, William Johnson took Brandt on a trip to England for Brandt in 1775 to form an alliance between the Mohawk and the British.

Joseph Brandt had left New York in company with Sir William Johnson on November 11, 1775. He arrived in

London sometime around December 12. Brandt dined with Colonel Arent DePeyster, a prominent agent in recruiting Indians in the British struggle with the colonists. After his meal, Brandt departed to London where he would remain until May 1775 conferring with British officials and the King.

Revolutionary War

During his stay there, he met King George II twice, as well as other English dignitaries. He allied his tribe with the British for the promise of land for the tribe in Quebec. The three thousand warriors that the alliance promised the British was a valuable asset. On November 11, 1778 he led a force that attacked, and destroyed, a village called Cherry Valley in New York. The ensuing massacre sparked the later Sullivan Expedition that would lay waste to nearly forty Iroquois villages.

Late July 1793 - Grand Council Meets with United States Commissioners

The Council at the Rapids of the Maumee consisted of three factions. The Shawnee and Miami, led by Simon Girty, insisted that the United States recognize the Treaty of Fort Stanwix, signed in 1784, that set the border between the United States and the Indian nations at the Ohio River. They also maintained that the United States must remove all forts and settlements north of the Ohio River. The United States maintained that it would be too expensive to remove the settlers. The Six Nations Tribes, led by Joseph Brandt, tried, without success, to moderate the council. During the days of the council William Wells was circulating through the various Indian camps gathering intelligence for General Wayne.

Mid May, 1793 - Joseph Brandt Meets with John Graves Simcoe

In a bid to help negotiate a peace, Mohawk leader Joseph Brandt began making preparations to travel to the meeting place between the natives and the Americans. On the way, he stopped to discuss the situation with British Lieutenant Governor John Graves Simcoe.

John Graves Simcoe (February 25, 1752 – October 26, 1806)

The Meeting

Simcoe had received a set of 1786 maps drawn up by British Governor at the time Sir William Johnson. The maps provided strong evidence that the boundary between the Indian tribes and the American settlements in Kentucky to be the Ohio River. Brandt studied the maps, and took them, hoping they would provide the Indian tribes with some strong ammunition in the coming council at Sandusky. Brandt had become convinced that the Indians would ultimately lose any war between the united tribes and that peace was the only way to preserve the Indian way of life.

July 07, 1793 - Indian Delegation Meets with Commissioners

A deputation of fifty Indian chiefs from the nations meeting at Sandusky arrived at Niagara-On-The-Lake on July 7.

The Indians Fears and Positions

Their purpose was to solidify their demand that the boundary between the Indian nations and the Americans had to be the Ohio River and that they would accept no American settlements north of the river. They questioned whether the commissioners had the authority to set the boundary at the Ohio River, as the assembled nations desired. They also expressed concern over the force that General Wayne had assembled in Indian Territory and the road he was building into the heart of their territory. Joseph Brandt acted as the mediator and translator during the council. The chiefs related that the following tribes had assembled at Sandusky and were in conference:

Mohawk

Onondaga

Oneida

Cayuga

Seneca

Wyandotte

Shawnee

Delaware

Muncie

Miami

Ottawa

Chippewa

Pottawattamie

Mingo

Cherokee

Nanticoke's

The representatives of the tribes made clear that the numbers and tribes changed daily as new representatives arrived.

The Commissioners Position

Benjamin Lincoln, speaking for the commissioners, expressed his regrets that the United States had felt it necessary to assemble a military force and the President Washington had forbidden Wayne to take up hostilities against the natives unless they were attacked first. Secondly, they made it known that they did have the authority to set the boundary, however they were sure that both parties would have to make compromises during the negotiations.

Confusion

Somehow, the Americans got the impression that the natives were willing to make compromises on the settlements already in existence. They offered money and trade goods in compensation for the lands that they had settled upon. The meetings would go on for three days, after which the natives agreed to accompany the commissioners to Sandusky to continue the talks.

Late July 1793 - Brandt Meets With Indians at Sandusky

The Indian delegation departed Niagra-On-The-Lake soon after the conference and returned to Sandusky to confer with the tribes gathered there. Brandt joined them at Sandusky and tried to convince them to accept an alternate border other than the Ohio. The natives refused. British agent Alexander McKee had joined the assemblage and told the chiefs that the British would supply them with arms and ammunition if they resisted. The Creek and Cherokee delegation that had arrived from the south urged the assembled Wabash tribes not to accept any compromise. The chiefs sent a message to the commissioners demanding that the Ohio River would be the border between the Americans and the Wabash tribes. Thus, the conference was in confusion over what course of action the natives should take. Meanwhile, at Hobson's Choice, General Wayne continued training his army.

May 26, 1792 - Heckeweller Departs Bethlehem

John Heckeweller departed Bethlehem, Pennsylvania on his way to Pittsburg to meet General Rufus Putnam and accompany him to Vincennes in the Northwest Territory to conduct peace negotiations with the Indian tribes of the Wabash.

June 1792

June 01, 1792 - Kentucky Becomes State

On June 1, 1792, Kentucky became the fifteenth state in the Union, following Vermont's lead. Vermont had become the fourteenth state on March 4, 1791.

June 02, 1792 - William Henry Harrison Promoted to Lieutenant

Harrison arrived at Fort Washington sometime during St. Clair's disastrous campaign in early November 1791. During the early stages of General James Wilkinson's temporary command of Fort Washington in St. Clair's absence, Harrison had accompanied him on his uneventful expedition to the battleground in January 1792. General Wilkinson next decided that another garrison was necessary in the chain of forts that St. Clair had established, so he had another one constructed, which he called Fort. St. Clair. This fort was near Eaton, Ohio, almost due north of Cincinnati and west of Dayton, near the Indiana/Ohio state line. Harrison served as commander of the guard every other night and gradually gained the favor of General Wilkinson.

Military Policeman

An incident in the growing city of Cincinnati proved providential for Harrison's future military career. Wilkinson had given permission for the soldiers to visit town during their off hours as long as they secured their commanding officer's permission. Soon incidents involving drunken soldiers drew complaints from the town's residents. The general issued orders stating that any soldier observed acting drunk and disorderly would be punished immediately with fifty lashes. Wilkinson sent squads of military police officers to enforce this edict and Harrison, as a junior officer, received assignment to this duty. He discovered two men from the fort that were drunk, so Harrison had their shirts stripped and then had them whipped. All through the incident, the man and his companion protested that they were civilian contractors to the army. They were not soldiers. Harrison paid no attention to their protests and proceeded with the punishment. The enraged men filed charges against Harrison, leading Wilkinson to search for a reason to get Harrison out of town. Wilkinson wanted to send his wife and children back east and used the occasion to get Harrison out of Cincinnati by sending him as an escort with his family. He was to take them as far as Philadelphia and then return.

Snared by General Wayne

Harrison reached Pittsburg and reported to the new commander in chief of the army, General Anthony Wayne. Wayne procured horses for Wilkinson's family and dispatched Wayne to continue his escort service of the family to Philadelphia, which he did. After his return to Fort Pitt, Wayne did not send Harrison back to Fort Washington. He liked Harrison and kept him at Fort Pitt to help train the army he needed to train. His later service to Wayne led him to promote him to lieutenant, which he made retroactive to June 2, 1792.

June 08, 1792 - Heckeweller Arrives Pittsburg

John Heckeweller arrived at Pittsburg on June 3, 1792. His party had crossed the mountains during a heat wave, causing Heckeweller to imbibe copious quantities of water. He was ill when he arrived, unable to keep food down and sick with a slight fever. In spite of this, he met with Rufus Putnam, who had arrived the day before. Putnam showed Heckeweller his instructions from Knox and the two men conferred. Rumors swirled over Indian activity in the area and reports of a band of over 100 warriors lurking in the area caused much alarm. A scouting party returned to the fort accompanied by several natives they had captured and some scalps the soldiers had taken arrived during Heckeweller and Putnam's conference. The men agreed to send the captives on to friendly Indians Cornstalk and some peaceful natives that had converted to the Moravian religion. These with the purpose of having them forward them on to the hostile Indians with some of the Moravians carrying messages of peace. Heckeweller had visited the fort's doctor, whose remedies cured him and he was ready to depart for Vincennes by June 8.

June 08, 1792 - Heckeweller and Putnam Depart on Peace Mission

John Heckweller and Rufus Putnam departed from Fort Pitt on June 8 to begin their mission of peace to the Wabash Indians. Traveling overland, they reached Washington, Pennsylvania in Washington County by evening, where they spent the night with Heckeweller's friend, a Mr. van Sweringen. From van Sweringen, They learned that the hostile Indians had murdered the Moravian Indians they had sent as emissaries. They had murdered them while they were praying, singing and kissing. He stated that he had heard the tale from the "very lips of the murderers."

Washington, Pennsylvania

Heckeweller notes that at the time of his visit, Washington was a town with about sixty well built houses, a stone courthouse and jail. The Pennsylvania General Assembly had created Washington County on March 28, 1781. The county seat, also named Washington, originally bore the name of Catfish Camp. The name derives from the French name ("Wissameking") which means "catfish place." The Delaware tribe had a village on a branch of Chartiers Creek which bore the name Catfish Camp. The Pennsylvania

Legislature deemed that the first elections in the county would take place at Catfish Camp. Washington County was the first county in the United States named in honor of General George Washington. Historical lore relates that the General had once stayed overnight at the site, however there is no record that Washington was ever in the area. The town had been the center of the Whiskey Rebellion just a year before. Surveyors began platting the town of Washington soon after the legislature created the county.

June 09, 1792 - Heckeweller and Putnam Reach Charlestown

Continuing on overland, Heckweller and Putnam reached Charlestown, now in West Virginia, on June 9. Heckeweller reports that the town, settled about four years before, contained about twenty houses with more lots for sale. The town had developed a prosperous trade in goods traveling along the Ohio River. The land part of their journey ended at Charlestown where they left their horses in the care of a wealthy farmer that would allow them to graze in the men's absence. They boarded a barge that the United States Government had sent to their demarcation point along with three men from Marietta and a detachment of soldiers. By late morning they reached Wheeling.

Wheeling

Heckewelder noted that they ate breakfast in Wheeling, also now in West Virginia. Town founder Ebenezer Zane advertised the 3/4 acre lots at prices ranging between $25.00 and $50. At Wheeling they met with Major William McMahon, a member of the Second Legion of the United States Army. McMahon had just returned from an expedition into native lands. The two held a meeting during which McMahon related the conditions of the Moravian settlements along the Muskingum River.

Hostile Native Meeting Sites

Major McMahon had found a meeting site for three hostile native tribes at a point where Gekelemukpechunk Creek empties into the Muskingum River. He found three distinct camps as well as three tall, painted war posts. Continuing on to Martin's Station After meeting with Major McMahon, Heckeweller and his party continued on, reaching Martin's Station at the mouth of the Muskingum River late in the day. On the approach to Marietta, the passengers on the barge passed two hostile Indians who fled as the vessel passed. The residents kept thirteen large, vicious dogs to warn them of Indian attack and provide some defense.

Moravian Settlements

The Moravians had established three settlements in what is now southeaster Ohio along and in the region of the Muskingum River in 1772. These settlements were Gnadenhutten, Schoenbrunn and Salem. Many natives in this region listened to the Moravian missionaries, which had included Heckweller and David Zeisburger, and converted to Christianity. During the Revolutionary War these peaceful natives, many of whom belonged to the Delaware tribe, stayed neutral in the war. The British had managed to recruit most of the other tribes to their cause. The British and the unconverted tribes distrusted the Moravian converts. The British removed the native population of Gnadenhutten in 1781 and imprisoned them near Detroit. After removing them, the British destroyed all the cabins and other improvements to the land that the natives had accomplished. The British allowed about a hundred to return in the fall to harvest their crops. These Delaware resettled the town, however in March a band of Pennsylvania militia that had entered the area looking for Indians that had been conducting raids in that state found the Delaware. They mistook them for the Indians that had been raiding and murdered ninety-six Delaware in an incident that has become known as the Gnadenhutten Massacre on March 8, 1782.

June 11, 1792 - Heckeweller and Putnam Reach Marietta

Heckeweller and Putnam's party would stay at Marietta for several days, thus the men spent some time exploring the settlement and the surrounding area, which consisted of three different fortifications. The Fortifications were Fort Harmar, Picketed Point Stockade and about three-quarters of a mile upstream from the Ohio on the Muskingum, Campus Martius.

War

The war between the Indians and the whites had prevented the setters from leaving the protection of the forts. They established farms, gristmills, a sawmill, a distillery, storehouses and other necessities of pioneer life. They did not live in the farms or businesses they established for fear of Indian attack. This was for good reason, as the day before Heckweller's party had arrived warriors had killed and scalped a man as he worked his fields within view of the settlement.

Fort Harmar

Constructed by the United States Army in the fall of 1785, Fort Harmar's original purpose was to keep white settlers from colonizing native lands. Located at the mouth of the Muskingum River on west bank, the pentagon-shaped fort featured horizontal log walls with bastions to help support them. Four palisades offered an elevated field of vision for defenders. Two story buildings inside the fort provided quarters for officers and men. The arsenal was in a tower that doubled as a watchtower.

Picketed Point Stockade

Constructed on the east side of the Muskingum River in 1791 directly across from Fort Harmar, Picketed Point Stockade comprised about four acres of land and four blockhouses.

Campus Martius

Constructed on an elevated plain on the remains of an old Indian mound, the fort was a short distance upriver from the Ohio River on the Muskingum River. Construction on the fort began in 1788 and concluded in 1791. Located on the east side of the Muskingum River the square fort had a blockhouse on each corner and stood thirty feet above the river. The fort included a seventy foot deep well, lined with bricks.

Productive Settlers

The settlers had cleared about 700 acres of land on which they planted orchards, vegetable gardens, vineyards and corn fields. The previous year the productive fields had sold over 10,000 bushels of surplus Indian corn to the commissary. Most farms had bee hives, chickens and pigs. The pigs produced about 4,000 pounds of lard per year. Because the Indians stole horses, the settlers had few of them, using oxen to perform most of the work. The sawmill sawed boards up to thirty-six inches wide from the huge trees cut down in the surrounding forests. The settlement had nine stores, two gristmills one of which was powered by oxen. Three inns provided quarters and food for travelers. Heckeweller's party stayed until June 26, when they moved on down the river towards Fort Washington.

General Benjamin Tupper Funeral

During their stay at Marietta, Heckeweller and Putnam attended the funeral of General Benjamin Tupper on June 17, who died the day before. He describes, in detail, a Masonic funeral with all its pomp and ceremony.

Benjamin Tupper (March 11, 1738 - June 16, 1792)

Thomas Tupper, IV and Remembrance Perry Tupper, Benjamin was native to Stoughton, Norfolk County, Massachusetts. His father died when he was a year old. A Boston tanner took him on as an apprentice until 1754, after which he began working as a farm hand. In 1756 he enlisted in the militia and served with the British during the French and Indian War. During this period he also ran a district school in Easton, Massachusetts. Tupper married Huldah White in 1762, with whom he had four children. After their marriage, the couple moved to Chesterfield, Massachusetts. At Chesterfield he enlisted in the militia, serving as a lieutenant.

Revolutionary War

Tupper joined the militia units that participated in the Battles of Lexington and Concord and became part of the force besieging Boston. On July 31 he led his company on a raid on Brewster's Island ten days after the Battle of Brewster Island.

July 31, 1775 - Battle of Brewster Island

The Boston Light was a lighthouse that aided navigators in their approach to Boston Harbor, leading General George Washington to order a raid to extinguish the light on July 21.

The Raid

This raid was successful, with the colonials taking the oil lamps and the oil they used for fuel. Before departing, they burned the wooden parts of the lighthouse. The raiders managed to elude a British warship that attempted to intercept them. The British sent a detachment of soldiers to guard the light and carpenters to repair the wooden parts of the lighthouse.

Second Raid

General Washington ordered Major Benjamin Tupper to lead a raid to destroy it again. Major Tupper assembled a force of 300 men and sailed from Dorchester and Squantum, Massachusetts on a flotilla of whaleboats. The Americans landed on the island and quickly defeated the 32 British soldiers that guarded the island. They took the British survivors of the skirmish and ten carpenters prisoner, after which they destroyed the repairs the carpenters had finished and returned to their whaleboats.

Battle of Brewster Island

While the colonials were employed capturing the British and destroying the repairs the tide went out, stranding the whaleboats. While Tupper's men tried to pull the boats back into the water, British reinforcements arrived and the battle began. Tupper's men prevailed and they escaped with only one man killed during the short, sharp battle. One of the British whaleboats sank, thus the British took heavier casualties than their American attackers.

June 11, 1792 - Shawnee and Delaware Warriors Raid Fort Jefferson

A small band of about 15 Shawnee and Delaware warriors attacked a detachment of 20 soldiers who were away from the fort cutting hay for their livestock. The warriors killed four of the soldiers in the attack and took the remainder captive. They killed 11 of the soldiers later and carried the remainder as captives to a Chippewa village. The frequent attacks on soldiers while out performing this necessary chore led General James Wilkinson to fear that the soldiers would not be able to gather sufficient hay for the animals.

June 25, 1792 – Hay Cutter's Massacre

On June 25, 1792 a detail of sixteen soldiers from Fort Jefferson sent out to cut hay for the livestock in the fort drew the attention of Simon Girty. Girty and about 100 warriors attacked the soldiers, killing or wounding the entire detail.

June 26, 1792 - Heckeweller and Putnam Depart Marietta

General Putnam and John Heckeweller departed Marietta on the morning of June 26, 1792 as they continued their journey to Vincennes. The barge contained a complement of nine men, including Heckeweller, Putnam and nine men traveling to Gallipolis. By evening they reached the settlement of Belle Prairie, or Belpre where they spent the night at the home of Major Nathan Goodale in Farmer's Castle.

Belpre

Established on April 11, 1789 as the second organized settlement in the Northwest Territory, Belpre was part of the Ohio Company's land purchase. The pioneers built Farmer's Castle in 1791 to protect them from Indian attack. Bathsheba Rouse became the first recorded woman teacher in the Northwest Territory when she opened a school in Farmer's Castle in 1791. In the fall of the same year a floating mill was built that used the Ohio River's current to grind corn into meal. The mill rested on two boats, one of which supported the grinding machinery and the other supported the shaft that turned the waterwheel. Rufus Putnam established the first circulating library in the Northwest Territory when he brought his book collection to the town in 1795.

Farmers' Castle Fort

About fifteen miles below Marietta on the Ohio River Farmers Castle on Backus Island (Blennerhasset Island), located in the middle of the Ohio River, to serve as a haven that protected them from Indian attack. The farmers began construction in the first week in January of 1791. The settlers used oxen teams to haul the logs, some a foot thick, to the site. The men dragged the smaller logs for the roof with ropes. They made door and window shutters with thick oak boards and barred them from the inside with heavy oak bars. The chinked the cracks between the logs with mortar and surrounded the blockhouses with a stockade built with oak logs. They built the stockade with fourteen foot long logs. They dug a four foot wide trench around the settlement to seat the logs. The stockade towered ten feet above the ground, with pointed ends, when complete. A layer of snow on the ground made dragging the logs easier. Families moved into the blockhouses as soon as they completed them. The fort consisted of thirteen blockhouses in two rows. A street ran between the blockhouses. The settlers abandoned the fort after General Anthony Wayne defeated the Indians at the Battle of Fallen Timbers in August 1794.

June 27, 1792 - Heckeweller and Putnam Arrive Gallipolis

During their journey down the Ohio River Heckeweller and Putnam passed the mouth of the Little Kanawa River, now the site of Parkersburg West Virginia. Heckeweller notes the existence of a spring that burned when exposed to fire, about fifteen miles above the river's mouth. The village that eventually sprang up near this spring became known as Burning Spring. By evening the expedition reached Gallipolis, where they stopped for a day.

Burning Spring

Natural gas escaping from pockets deep underground bubbled up through a spring that emptied into the Little Kanawa River. Captain Matthew Arbuckle, the Reverend J. Alderson, and John and Peter Van Bibber discovered the spring in 1773. The area around the mouth actually contained three of these oddities, which are not really springs. Instead, they are pockets in the ground near the river which filled with rainwater. When lit, the fire burned until the wind extinguished it, as it was nearly impossible for anyone to put it out. Historical lore indicates that the first man to discover its nature had gone to the spring with a lit torch at night and ignited the fumes of gas. The terrified hunter fled the site. Rathbone Well, acknowledged as the world's oldest oil well, is located in a thirty-one acre park which now marks the location of the springs and the oil complex that grew up there. Burning Springs Park, now listed by the National Register of Historic Places, includes a state historic marker that recounts the area's history.

June 28, 1792 - Heckeweller and Putnam in Gallipolis

Heckeweller and Putnam spent the day at Gallipolis admiring the craftsmanship of the French artisans that had relocated to the new city of Gallipolis.

Skilled Workers and Gardens

The men admired the creations of the goldsmiths, watchmakers and glass makers in the new town. Putnam purchased a watch and the two men bought a few items from the glassmaker, including a barometer, thermometer and a glass tobacco pipe. The artisans had developed a market for their crafts as far away as New Orleans at the southern tip of the Mississippi River. They admired the gardens of the town, which the inhabitants had laid out in a European style. The inhabitants had planted almond trees, vineyards, artichokes and some rice. The town also had a population of boat builders who constructed high quality boats. The population was about 400, living in about 150 houses.

Gallipolis - "The Old French City"

Founded on October 17, 1790 by French Immigrants fleeing the horrors of the French Revolution, the town of Gallipolis was the second settlement formed in the Northwest Territory. The name means the "City of the Gauls." The original settlers, known as the "The French 500," consisted of an assortment of French aristocrats, merchants, and artisans. These people had purchased land along the Ohio River from a land company known as the Scioto Company in 1789. The people left France, voyaging separately on several different ships. Most of these new settlers landed in Alexandria, Virginia. Once assembled, they traveled to their proposed settlement along the Ohio River. Upon arrival they learned that the deeds they had purchased were worthless, as the Scioto Company did not own the land they sold. These French people were not pioneers, they were settled city people. The rude conditions on the American frontier shocked them, but somehow they survived. They built their homes and a stockade for protection. At the time of Heckweller's visit these new settlers had built a settlement, gardens and established a thriving trade along the rivers. They had appealed to President George Washington for help and were awaiting word from the President.

June 30, Peace Expedition Reach Cincinnati

The expedition completed the voyage from Gallipolis to Cincinnati without incident. They passed the mouth of the Big Sandy River, the present border between West Virginia and Kentucky, where they sighted places where buffalo had drank water along the riverbank. During the night, a dense layer of fog enveloped them, which was fortunate. They had left the boat float along the river all night, with a guard posted, and passed the most dangerous point on the river, the mouth of the Scioto River, without incident. The mouth of the Scioto had been the site of many native attacks on boats that passed by, Heckeweller reports that about 150 people had died along that stretch of river. They passed Massie's Station at about 4:00 in the afternoon.

Massie's Station

Founded in 1790 by Nathanial Massie, the town was situated on the north side of the Ohio River near three islands in the Ohio River. Heckeweller records that at the time of his visit the largest island, about two miles long, had been completely planted in Indian corn. The residents renamed the town Manchester, its current name, in 1791. At the time of Heckeweller's visit about thirty families lived in the town, protected by a stockade. The fourth permanent settlement in the Northwest Territory, Manchester served as the home base for explorer/surveyor Nathanial Massie.

Nathanial Massie (December 28, 1763 - November 03, 1813)

The son of Nathaniel and Elizabeth Watkins Massie, Nathanial was native to Goochland County, Virginia. Nathaniel served in the Revolutionary War. In 1783 he migrated to Kentucky to farm land his father owned. Massie had studied surveying and began exploring lands north of the Ohio River in the Northwest Territory. In 1790 Massie surveyed the town that would become Manchester.

Continuing Downstream

About two hours later they passed Limestone, where they paused briefly to dine. They continued on, beginning about 9:00 PM and drifted downriver through the night. Contrary winds and a weak current allowed them to make only about twelve miles through the night. They passed a point called Ten-Mile Reach, so called because for the next ten miles the river followed a straight course bounded on both sides by low, flat banks, about 8:00 AM. By 5:00 PM they reached Columbia, where they docked for the night to stay with Major Benjamin Stites. After breakfasting with Major Stites the next morning, they departed and arrived at Cincinnati at about 9:00 AM, where they stopped. They would stay at the settlement for several days.

July 1792

July 03, 1793 - Heckeweller and Putnam Learn of Trueman's Fate

Upon arriving at Cincinnati, nine cannon shots rang out, announcing General Putnam's arrival. The men found that quarters in the fort had been secured for them; however, Heckeweller opted to stay with a resident named Martin in the town.

Indian Prisoners

After resting, the two men visited fifty-six Indian prisoners that had been held inside a stockade in the fort. These natives were of the Wawiachtenos tribe and lived along the Eel River in current Indiana. General James Wilkinson had captured them during his August 1791 mission to the region. These natives were scheduled to be released in a few days.

Original Mission

Putnam's original mission had been to hold initial negotiations with some of the native tribes at Fort Jefferson on July 1 before traveling on to Vincennes for more talks. Messengers had delivered the messages to the various tribes. General Wilkinson, the commander at Fort Washington, had gone on a mission to visit the forts in the chain General St. Clair had constructed the year before. He returned to Fort Washington around noon on July 2 and met with Putnam and Heckeweller. He reported that he had deployed several workmen near Fort Jefferson on July 1, with fifteen soldiers guarding them. A band of warriors had surrounded this group and either captured or killed all of them. Putnam and Heckeweller had intended to travel to Fort Jefferson to engage in negotiations; however the news of the massacre near the fort led them to conclude that the attack had been meant for them. This conclusion changed their minds and they decided to remain at Fort Washington until they learned the fate of the other peace missions led by Isaac Freeman and Alexander Trueman.

Trueman and Freeman's Fate Learned

Francis Vigo and Henry Vanderburgh arrived at Fort Washington on July 3 from Vincennes with five Wea tribesmen, led by Chief Jean Krouch, that were to accompany the freed prisoners back to Vincennes. Vigo and Vanderburgh reported that the Indians had said that they had seen the papers and wampum belts that had belonged to Freeman and Trueman displayed in their villages and that the men had been murdered.

Francis Vigo (1747 - March 22, 1836)

Native to Mondovi in northern Italy, historians know little of his early life. Disagreements with his parents led him to depart while young, for Spain. Vigo became a muleteer, a man who engaged in packing goods by mule back. Vigo joined a Spanish regiment and was sent to New Orleans. Upon completing his military enlistment, Vigo became a fur trader, a trade at which he became quite successful. Traveling to St. Louis, he became friends and a business associate of Spanish Lieutenant Governor Fernando de Leyba. Vigo made his headquarters at St. Louis and made frequent trips to the trading post at Vincennes. Vigo, no friends of the British, befriended Clark at his headquarters in Kaskaskia after Clark had captured the fort. in July 1778. Vigo lent both money and supplies to Clark to aid him when the expedition became short of both.

American Spy

British Lieutenant Colonel Hamilton led a force down the Wabash River and recaptured the post in December. Unaware that the British had recaptured the town, Vigo traveled to Vincennes in January, 1779. The British captured him. Not knowing he was an ardent supporter of the

Americans and had worked with Clark, the British released him after extracting a promise that he would do nothing to aid the Americans during his return trip. Honoring his pledge, he returned directly to St. Louis. After returning he traveled fifty miles to Kaskaskia to consult with Clark, informing him of the British strength and deployments at Vincennes. Clark immediately began planning his campaign to capture Vincennes.

Vincennes Resident

After the Revolutionary War ended, Vigo moved to Vincennes permanently. In Vincennes Vigo continued in the fur trade and from 1790 until 1810 he served in the Knox County militia. In 1818 the Indiana General Assembly established Vigo County, naming the new county in his honor. Vigo visited Terra Haute in 1834. The county treated him like the hero he was, feting him in almost royal style. Vigo's business affairs had taken an unfavorable turn and an almost impoverished Vigo died in 1836. He is interred in Greenlawn Cemetery in Vincennes. The United States Government had not paid Vigo for the aid he lent Clark during his momentous campaign during his lifetime. In 1876 the government finally compensated Vigo's estate. Vigo had stipulated in his will that his estate should be used to install a bell in the Vigo County Courthouse, the county named in honor of him. The funds, $8,616 principal and $41,282 in interest, were used to purchase and install a bell. In 1834 sculptor John Angel received a commission to sculpt a statue of Francis Vigo. The same year the

Vigo accompanied Heckeweller and Putnam on the journey from Fort Washington to Vincennes

July 04, 1792 - Joseph Shaylor Reinstated by By General Wayne

General Anthony Wayne reinstated Joseph Shaylor on July 4, 1792. Wayne charged Shaylor with transforming his regiment into a rifle company and at the beginning of October assigned him as commander of Fort St. Clair.

July 05, 1792 - Heckeweller Explores Cincinnati

Judge John Cleves Symmes had established Cincinnati on December 28, 1788, about three and a half years before Heckeweller and Putnam visited it. Symmes had established the city on a pleasant plain that extended about two miles along the bank of the river and penetrated about seven miles north of the river.

Heckeweller's Description

The river at this point had two banks, each about forty feet high. A lower town had developed along the second bank of the river and the upper town above that. Roads connected the two towns The town had 354 lots which had been purchased and occupied. Each lot included four acres outside of town that provided a garden for the settler to grow their food. Initially, the lots had sold for $8.00 to $12.00 each, however the demand made by incoming settlers had inflated the price of a lot to $30 to 60$ each, depending upon the location.

Red Houses

About 200 houses, each painted red, had been built. Many of these houses were two story houses. Rental fees on these houses ranged from $50 - $60 per year. At the center of town, two large squares had been reserved, one for a church and the other for a court house. The church was under construction and under roof. Heckeweller notes that the surveyed lots outside town had all been fenced off "with good posts."

Crops

The settlers had planted Indian corn, turnips, wheat, oats, millet, barley and potatoes.

Population

The city's population, at this point and not including the garrison at Fort Washington, numbered about 900 people. Fort Washington, its palisades painted red, towered over the city on the east end. The garrison of the fort at the time of Heckeweller's visit, numbered about 200.

Government

The city had its own judges and held court regularly. The military desired to govern the city, but the citizens had held firm to their Constitutional rights and kept their government.

Merchants

The city had an overabundance of merchants, which led to an overabundance of goods, with over thirty warehouses. The abundance of goods had led to a tough market for the merchants, as prices were too low. He also reports that the city was overrun with idle people that created problems for the other citizens. Many hoped that as soon as law enforcement improved that these would desert the city for other places.

Beautiful Area

Heckeweller noted the beauty of the area around Cincinnati, adding that the Licking River that emptied into the Ohio from Kentucky enhanced the magnificent scenery. A city called Newport had been established across from Cincinnati at the mouth of that river. Two ferries operated, carrying goods and passengers across the Ohio River. At Newport a road led south to Lexington, which at that time was the capital of Kentucky.

July 12, 1792 - William Wells Arrives at Cincinnati

During the interval of Heckeweller's tour of Cincinnati and the arrival of William Wells, Heckeweller reports two attacks by Indians.

The First Attack

The first occurred on July 7 when two men, a woman and a boy traveled to Columbia in a canoe. About a mile and a half from Cincinnati a band of Indians attacked. They shot the two men, one of which died, and captured the boy. One of the men died, whom the warriors scalped. The other, wounded, eluded them. The woman became frightened during the attack and fell into the river. The current carried her away from the scene of the attack and she made her way to shore and took the news back to Cincinnati. The militia traveled to the scene to rescue the wounded man and recover the body of the dead man, whose head was mangled. After cutting the musket ball from the wounded man's shoulder, the doctor declared him safe.

The Second Attack

On July 8 heavy rain fell in the Ohio River Valley which had raised the river level by about eleven feet on July 9. The river's rise allowed several flatboats which had been waiting at Pittsburg for higher water to depart. When they passed the mouth of the Scioto, a band of Indians attacked, firing into the flatboats. A large number of them entered their canoes and began rowing out to the flatboats to kill the crew and take the boats; however boats coming up from behind were well armed and fired several hot volleys into them, driving them off. The flatboats continued their voyage to Cincinnati without further incident.

William Wells (c. 1770 – August 15, 1812)

The youngest son of Samuel Wells and Ann Farrow Wells, William was a native of Jacob's Creek, Pennsylvania. The family migrated down the Ohio River by flatboat in 1779, landing at Louisville, Kentucky. Anne died soon after they arrived. In September 1781 Samuel died in a Miami raid called Long Run massacre. Louisville resident William Pope took the boy in. In 1784 William and three other boys went on a camping trip near the Ohio River at Robert's Pond. A band of Miami Indians captured the boys. After his capture the Miami took him to an Amerindian village on the Eel River in northern Indiana called Kenapakomoko.

Adoption by the Miami

Gaviahate, the "Porpucine," the village chief adopted Samuel, who adapted well to Miami life. He became a skilled hunter and warrior. The Miami called him Apekonit (carrot) because of his red hair. He took part in many raids on white settlements, sometimes serving as a decoy to lure the targets into a false sense of security. He married a Miami woman and together they had a child. General James Wilkinson raided their village while William was absent on a raid. His wife and child disappeared during the raid, presumably killed. William then married Wanagapeth or Sweet Breeze, the daughter of Little Turtle. The two would have four children.

Contact with his Brother

On a trading venture to Vincennes in 1789, William met his brother Samuel. The two traveled together to Fort Nelson, where William warned the fort's commander General Rufus

Putnam that the British were trying to incite the natives into attacking the Americans.

William Wells

William Wells arrived in Cincinnati on July 12 to act as an interpreter for Putnam during his negotiations with the Indians at Vincennes. William Wells arrived in Cincinnati on July 12.

Henry Vanderburgh (1760–1812)

The son of William Vanderburgh and Margaret Gay, Henry was a native of Troy, New York. On November 21, 1776 John Jay, as a member of New York City's legislative body, the Committee of One Hundred, appointed Vanderburgh a Lieutenant in the 5th New York Regiment of the Continental Army. Jay later commissioned him as a captain in the 2nd Regiment. Vanderburgh served throughout the Revolutionary War. He migrated to the Indiana Territory and served as a territorial judge until he died in 1812. His grave is near Vincennes.

July 14, 1792 - Messengers Arrive from Fort Jefferson

On July 14 a special messenger arrived at Fort Washington with the news that two soldiers had deserted during a work detail and taken prisoner by the Indians. The natives released the men, who were then recaptured by a detachment of light cavalry.

Messengers Killed

A judge at the fort put them under oath and they testified they had seen scalps, clothing, papers and belts belonging to Isaac Freeman and Alexander Trueman. The warriors stated that they had killed these peace messengers and they would kill all others. They asserted that they would not negotiate until all the Americans abandoned their forts and settlements on the north side of the Ohio River. Until the Americans did that, all messengers and deserters would meet the same fate.

Girty Involved in Attack

From the messenger General Wilkinson also learned that Simon Girty had been involved in the June 25 attack on Fort Jefferson and that the natives had driven all the cattle away from the pens at the fort. The soldiers and workers reported seeing Indians in the vicinity of the fort every day. News arrived from Columbia that a band of thirty Indians had captured three men near the fort and escaped. Pursuit by a detachment of cavalry soldiers had been fruitless, as the Indians fled through a swamp about forty miles from the fort. The horses could not travel through the swamp, thus they had to abandon the rescue mission.

July 16, 1792 - Chief Jean Krouch Died

Chief Jean Krouch had arrived with Francis Vigo and Henry Vanderburgh on July 3 in company with four other members of the Wea tribe.

Jean Krouch (? - July 16, 1792)

Chief Jean Krouch had led a delegation of Wea Indians from Vincennes to Cincinnati to accompany a number of natives that General Charles Scott had captured on his expedition in May and June of 1791. The members of the tribe had authorized Chief Krouch with a great deal of power to negotiate a treaty and free the captives. Unfortunately, Krouch died suddenly on July 16, 1792 at Cincinnati.

July 17, 1792 - Chief Jean Krouch Funeral

Acting Governor Winthrop Sargent, acting in the place of the absent Governor St. Clair, authorized a full military funeral for Chief Jean Krouch and allowed his burial in the fort's cemetery. Almost the entire body of Indian prisoners and their visitors followed the body's procession to the grave, one of them carrying a white flag on a pole. An honor guard fired three volleys of shots over the grave. After interring the body they natives planted the white flag at the head of the grave.

Grave Desecrated

During the night someone dug up the body, tore down the flag and stamped it in the mud. The dragged the body along the muddy street and stood it up along it. Sargent had the body re-interred, a new flag put up. He also offered a $100 reward for the names of the perpetrators. He posted the reward as a proclamation nailed on a post near the grave. The next night someone tore down the second flag, but did not bother the body. They did tear down the proclamation with the reward. The third night, Sargent had a guard posted near the grave, which ended the problem.

July 19, 1792 - Indian Prisoners Confer with Putnam

The chief of the Indian prisoners conferred with General Rufus Putnam on July 19, asking him to accompany them when they traveled to Vincennes. He implored Putnam to allow them to travel soon because he was afraid that more of them would die if they stayed at Fort Washington. Putnam informed him that he had delayed their journey for thirty days.

July 22, 1792 - Letter from Rufus Putnam to Secretary Knox

On July 22, 1792 General Rufus Putnam dispatched a letter to Secretary of War Henry Knox in which he relates the news from William Wells and the Indians from Vincennes that the messengers of peace have failed. Wells and the Indians reported that Trueman and Freeman had been murdered by the Indians. He indicated that he did not believe that any of the tribes would come to Fort Washington to confer. Putnam proposed traveling to Port Vincent (Vincennes) to investigate whether any of the tribes would confer with him and sign a treaty. He informed the Secretary that he would wait until August 15 before departing with the Indian prisoners and that General Wilkinson had agreed to send a company of troops as protection for his mission. Putnam hoped that he would receive encouraging news from Captain Hendrick in the interval of the letter and his departure date.

July 22, 1792 - Soldier Punished for Rebellion

A soldier that tried to incite a rebellion had the verdict the punishment inflicted upon him for trying to incite a rebellion. His head was shaved and he was forced to run the gauntlet. After this, they tied a horse collar around his neck and drummed him out of the fort.

July 29, 1773 - First Schoolhouse in Ohio Completed Schoenbrunn Ohio

David Zeisberger and his band of twenty-eight Moravians arrived in May, 1772 to establish a village they would call Schoenbrunn. Schoenbrunn was the first Christian settlement in the region that would become the State of Ohio.

Moravian Church

The Moravians are one of the oldest Protestant Christian churches in the world, dating from about 1457 in Bohemia. Reformer Jan Hus disagreed with several practices in the Catholic Church and started the Hussite movement that evolved into the Moravian Church. In 1722 members of the church fled to Saxony to escape religious persecution. They established a settlement in Germany called Herrnhut. From this village the Moravians started the first international missionary movement, establishing settlements in many countries.

The Moravian School

The first efforts at settlement involved building cabins, planting gardens for food and hunting the nearby forests for game. By spring 1773 the settlers build a school, which they completed on July 29, 1773. The schoolmaster taught both Moravian boys and girls, unusual for a colonial school. The school also taught native converts. The Moravians had printed a bible in the Delaware (Lenape) language so their native converts could read scripture.

Marriage and Author

He married Sarah Ohneberg in 1780, with whom he would have three children. After his marriage, Heckeweller continued his mission. The British arrested Heckeweller and Zeisburger, trying them for treason on November 3, 1781. They were exonerated. Over the ensuing years, Heckeweller continued his work among the Indians, trying to make peace and convert them.

David Zeisberger (April 11, 1721 – November 17, 1808)

The son of David and Rosina Zeisberge, David was native to Zauchtenthal, Moravia (present day Suchdol nad Odrou,

Czech Republic.) His parents migrated to the Colony of Georgia in the New World while David was a boy; however, David remained in Europe to complete his education. He rejoined his family in Savannah, Georgia in 1738. The Zeisberger family had begun working among the Creek Indians in Georgia, hoping to convert them to Christianity. David moved to Pennsylvania to help the church establish the settlements of Bethlehem and Nazareth. He received his ordination as a minister in 1749, after which he began missionary efforts among the Delaware tribe. During his missionary work, he became an advocate for the rights of the native tribes.

Partnership with David Zeisburger

In 1771 David Zeisburger traveled to Bethlehem and requested that Heckeweller join him in his quest to found Moravian missions on the frontier. The men founded the first settlement in Ohio, Schoenbrunn, in 1772, and the first school in 1773.

Schoenbrunn Village

The Delaware Indian chief Netawatwes invited Zeisberger to found a village in along the Tuscarawas River in the Ohio Country in 1772. Zeisberger and several Delaware families moved into the area, found a suitable site and founded their village. The villagers built cabins and planted gardens that included corn, beans, squash, potatoes and turnips. The built the first school house in Ohio and established the first civil code. the council consisted of Zeisberger, several Moravians and Delaware converts. The Delaware established the rules for the settlement. The village prospered for several years; however the tensions created by the Revolutionary War proved too great and by 1777 the villagers abandoned the settlement. Schoenbrunn Village has been restored. Those interested in visiting the restored village may contact:

Schoenbrunn Village

1984 E. High Avenue

New Philadelphia, OH 44663

800.752.2711

https://www.ohiohistory.org/visit/museum-and-site-locator/schoenbrunn-village

July 29, 1773 - First Schoolhouse in Ohio Completed Schoenbrunn Ohio

David Zeisberger and his band of twenty-eight Moravians arrived in May, 1772 to establish a village they would call Schoenbrunn. Schoenbrunn was the first Christian settlement in the region that would become the State of Ohio.

Moravian Church

The Moravians are one of the oldest Protestant Christian churches in the world, dating from about 1457 in Bohemia. Reformer Jan Hus disagreed with several practices in the Catholic Church and started the Hussite movement that evolved into the Moravian Church. In 1722 members of the church fled to Saxony to escape religious persecution. They established a settlement in Germany called Herrnhut. From this village the Moravians started the first international missionary movement, establishing settlements in many countries.

The Moravian School

The first efforts at settlement involved building cabins, planting gardens for food and hunting the nearby forests for game. By spring 1773 the settlers build a school, which they completed on July 29, 1773. The schoolmaster taught both Moravian boys and girls, unusual for a colonial school. The school also taught native converts. The Moravians had printed a bible in the Delaware (Lenape) language so their native converts could read scripture.

August 1792

August 06, 1792 - Indians Attack

Indians attacked a group of settlers traveling from Columbia to Dunlop's Station, killing one and wounding another.

August 11, 1792 - Military Supplies Arrive at Fort Washington

A flotilla of four flatboats arrived at Fort Washington from Fort Pitt bearing military supplies.

August 13, 1792 - Indian Attack Three Sites

Indian warriors staged three separate attacks on August 13, 1792, Fort St. Clair, Dunlop's Station and Fort Hamilton. At Fort St. Clair they shot through a soldier's hat, who was unharmed aside from needed a new hat. At Fort Hamilton natives stole seventeen horses, however the soldiers that owned the horses, Kentucky militia serving at the fort, pursued the thieves, shot and killed one and retrieved the horses. The attack at Dunlop's Station was more serious. The raiders shot three men, wounding them. One, soldier died.

August 16, 1792 - Prisoners Travel to Vincennes

On August 16, 1792 General James Wilkinson released the Indian prisoners and placed them on four barges guarded by the sixty soldier escort that had arrived a few days before. The officer in charge of the release and transport informed Mr. Heckeweller that the interment of the Indians had cost the government over $60,000. William Wells, acting as interpreter, had departed with them. Upon their departure, General Rufus Putnam dispatched a letter to Secretary of War Henry Knox informing him of the departure and expressing his hope that the release would display the United States' good faith and result in the gathering of 700 natives at Vincennes to conclude a peace treaty and bring peace.

August 18, 1792 - Putnam and Heckeweller Depart for Vincennes

Two days after the Indian prisoners departed from Fort Washington, John Heckeweller and General Rufus Putnam boarded their raft and began their long journey down the Ohio River to Vincennes.

Passengers

Passengers on the voyage included Francis Vigo and Henry Vanderburgh, who had accompanied the Wea chiefs that came to escort the released prisoners. A Captain Collins and Dr. Samuel Boyd would travel as far as Louisville, as both men had settled in the area. Seven miles into the trip they passed South Bend, on the north side of the river and eight miles beyond that North Bend, also on the north side of the Ohio River. Heckeweller notes that the settlement, founded by Judge John Symmes, had grown to 300 - 400 people and had not suffered an Indian attack in two years. Many of the settlers lived in the town and others lived on farms surrounding the settlement. Heckeweller and Putnam stopped for a brief visit.

The Eagle

Judge Symmes had made friends with the Indians that inhabitant the region, a practice that Heckeweller attributes to the lack of attacks on the settlement. He also described a Shawnee chief's observation of the United States emblem, the eagle, during a trading visit about three years prior. A large number of natives had visited the settlement in company with the chief. Symmmes had treated them well and given them many gifts. During a tour of the settlement, Symmes showed him the symbol of the United States, "Well," said a Shawanese captain, "let me also give my explanation, perhaps it will come nearer to the truth than yours. You tell me that every power has its own coat of arms and that this is good and useful. You have told me much of the peaceful intentions of the United States towards the Indians, and you show as a proof this picture. If the United States were such lovers of peace as you describe them to be, they would have chosen for their coat of arms something more appropriate and expressive of it. For example there are many good, innocent birds. There is the dove which would not do harm to the smallest creature. But what is the eagle? He is the largest of all birds and the enemy of all birds. He is proud, because he is conscious of his size and strength. On a tree, as well as in flight he shows his pride and looks down disparagingly upon all the birds. His head, his eyes, his beak and his long brown talons declare his strength and hostility. Now this bird, which is terrible enough in itself you have depicted as even more dreadful and horrible. You have not only put one of the implements of war, a bundle of arrows into one of his talons, and rods in the other, but have painted him in the most fearful manner, and in a position of attack upon his prey. Now tell me, have I not spoken the truth?"

Symmes had agreed with the observation, but also noted that only enemies of the United States needed to fear the eagle. Friends could look upon the symbol and see a symbol of protection, which the natives who had befriended the United States enjoyed.

Author Note: The preceding passage is copied directly from Heckeweller's journal.

First Night

The men continued on downriver, passing the Great Miami River's junction with the Ohio. Heckeweller notes great flocks of wild turkeys and geese along and on the Miami. They next passed Tanner's Station, on the Kentucky side of the River. They purchased butter and watermelons from settlers at the settlement, and then continued on. Heckeweller describes multitudes of wild fowl, deer and buffalo grazing along the river. At nightfall, they left the raft float in the current while they slept.

Provisions

The next morning, the 19th, they again saw great numbers of buffalo and deer along the river. Captain Collins shot one, and hit it. However when he embarked on the riverbank, he noted Indian tracks in the soft earth near the bank, and did not pursue the animal. Close to nightfall, Collins again shot a young cow buffalo, which weighed between 400 and 500 pounds. He managed to procure that one, which would provide plenty of meat for the travelers during the remainder of their trip. Once again, they left the barge drift with the current during the night. The next day, they reached Fort Steuben, near the Falls of the Ohio.

August 20, 1792   Heckeweller and Putnam Reach Fort Steuben

The next morning Heckeweller noted the buffalo and deer that grazed along the River. He observed many small settlements along the Ohio on the Kentucky side of the river. The party passed Twelve Mile Island and Six Mile Island, both covered with Carolina Reed, which also covers the regions swampy areas. By about 2:00 in the afternoon the party reached Fort Steuben, renamed from Fort Finney the previous year. The party of Indians with their sixty man guard unit had arrived the day before. At the arrival of General Putnam, the gunner of Fort Steuben fired nine cannon shots in his honor. The men slept in tents along the banks of the Ohio River that night surrounded by armed sentries.

Six Mile Island

Receiving its name from its distance from the Falls of the Ohio, Six Mile island is nearer the Indiana side of the river, however the Commonwealth of Kentucky owns the island and manages it as the Six Mile Island Nature Preserve. Accessible only by boat, the Preserve is noted for the vast numbers of water birds that inhabit it. During the annual Great Steamboat Race during the Kentucky Derby, the magnificent boats use the island as a turn around point. Kentucky dedicated the Preserve on June 24, 1979.

12 Mile Island

A short distance from Charlestown State Park, 12 Mile Island is owned by Jefferson County in Indiana and Oldham County in Kentucky. Boaters on the river have access to a ladder on the Kentucky side that allows access to the small island. General John Morgan attempted to cross the Ohio River near the Island in July 1863; however Union troops repelled his attack.

August 21, 1792 - The Putnam Party Traverses the Falls of the Ohio

The Putnam party camped below the Falls of the Ohio as a pilot hired for the fee of a guinea a day for each boat he guides down the great Falls. The boats dock first and men unload all the goods on them, load them on a wagon and transport them to a site below the Falls. One boat still had two Indians, who were sick, and two soldiers on board. Three of the boats ran aground while only one made it through by nightfall. During the night the boat that had the Indians and soldiers sank. The occupants managed to get on the roof of the boat, thus avoiding drowning in the raging current. The commander of the fort procured ropes and men to pull the boats free, so that by nightfall the boats all anchored at the lower end of the Falls, as well as three additional boats loaded with supplies for Fort Vincennes. One boat's rudder broke and needed repair, so the party camped at the Falls for several days as this was done.

August 22, 1792 - Heckeweller's Description of the Falls

The Putnam party spent four days camped at the Falls, during which Heckeweller and tow army officers toured the falls.

Three Channels

Heckeweller describes them as having three channels, a south, north and middle. Each channel's character was quite different. The river passed over a series of rocky steps on the south channel. The rocks are smooth and pointed in this channel. He describes the middle channel as flowing like a mill stream, fast and turbulent. The north channel flowed with a furious current over treacherous rapids. Boats could pass over the falls safely during high water, but during low water the voyage was slow and treacherous.

Fossils

He describes the rocky bed as having the petrified skeletons of many fish and animals that resisted efforts of the curious traveler to pick them up. At the time the people believed that any animal caught on the rocky bed during low water became petrified. Thus he describes what we know as fossils today that are millions of years old.

Fort Steuben and Clarksville

He relates that both shores of the river contain immense stands of cottonwood trees and that below the falls; men catch bounteous numbers of rockfish. During the summer months wild geese appear in great numbers swim on the calm, deep waters below the falls. Here great numbers of fish perish, providing food for the inhabitants pigs, which forage near the banks. Heckeweller reports that Fort Steuben, called Fort Finney by Kentucky residents, is on the upper end and north side of the falls, garrisoned with sixty soldiers. The town of Clarksville, established by General George Rogers Clark in 1783, also lies on the north side on the lower end of the falls.

Louisville

Heckeweller also visited a few residents in Louisville, which he describes as having about 150 houses. It was on a low plateau and had two highways leading to other Kentucky towns. The region on the Kentucky side had become well settled, with Louisville, along with Lexington to the southeast, being considered as sites for the future capital of Kentucky. Heckeweller reports that a committee would visit the growing town in three weeks to decide its fate. He named the thick fogs that formed there from the rushing waters of the falls as the only disadvantage. The people at the time people believed that the various mosquito borne fevers that afflicted those near the water were caused by the fog. During his stay, Heckeweller received several invitations from Louisville residents to stay in their houses, however he elected to stay camped at the base of the falls with his companions. By August 26, the boats repairs had been completed and the company continued its journey.

August 26, 1792 - The Putnam Party Departs

On August 26 the party of 160 Indians and soldiers accompanied by Putnam, Heckeweller, Wells, Vanderburgh and other assorted travelers boarded four Kentucky boats, three barges and several canoes to continue their voyage to the town of Vincennes.

Bountiful Country

The travelers journeyed through a country that abounded with game and never lacked for meat. From the banks of the Ohio River they saw multitudes of buffalo and deer from which the hunters could shoot and dress as many as they needed for sustenance. In addition to buffalo, on the 27th they shot two bears as well as a buffalo cow. By August 30 the company had passed the region of hills and entered the low, flat countryside between current Owensboro, Kentucky and Evansville, Indiana. On August 31 a stampeding herd of buffalo plunged into the river and almost overwhelmed the party as they passed near a large island. They did not shoot any of these animals, as they had plenty to do to avoid the animals' hooves as they thundered along. The same day they passed the Green River that enters the Ohio from Kentucky and approached the settlement of Red Bank, on the Kentucky side of the river.

September 1792

September 2, 1792 - The Putnam Party Reaches the Wabash River

The Putnam party passed Red Bank, Kentucky on August 31 and continued on their voyage until they reached the mouth of the Wabash, where the stopped and made camp a short distance down river.

Change of Boats

The party camped in a beautiful spot on a high bank overlooking Nine Mile Island, where they spotted some other white people camping as they inspected it with a spyglass. While they camped, the soldiers tore the barges and flatboats apart, as they were too large and unwieldy to make the voyage up the Wabash. Instead, they would sail on six large pirogues that the commanding officer of Vincennes had dispatched downriver and arrived on September 3. The soldiers used the wood from the boats they tore apart to build a fortification. The would leave a large quantity of the supplies at this spot, with a guard of twenty-five men, until they could send more boats down to get them. The pleasant spot pleased everyone, most of all General Putnam. He had a bounteous meal prepared for the three officers that had come down from Fort Vincennes, Heckeweller, Vanderburg and Vigo.. The meal consisted of buffalo, bear, turkey, deer, pork, pike, duck, turtle soup and several vegetables. Heckeweller noted that the noise of the flocks of Carolina parakeet, *Conuropsis carolinensis*, which existed in great numbers in a large area of the future United States and is now extinct, was "dreadful".

September 04, 1792 - The Putnam Party Begins Voyage up the Wabash

The flotilla of pirogues departed from the camp at the mouth of the Wabash on the afternoon of September 4. They traveled about eight miles upriver before disembarking and camping for the night. Heckeweller noted that the mood of the Indian prisoners lightened as they began the voyage up the Wabash, as they were now in their home territory. The voyage went smoothly until September 6, when Heckeweller became ill with a fever. At length he had to leave the pirogue and lie on the shore until a canoe came to get him to continue the journey to Vincennes. They arrived there on September 12.

September 04, 1792 - Anthony Wayne Announces the Formation of the Legion of the United States

On September 4, 1792, Major General Anthony Wayne, stationed in Pittsburg, announced the formation of the Legion of the United States. The Legion would consist of four sub-legions commanded by a brigadier-general.

September 12, 1792 - Putnam and Heckewelder Arrive Vincennes

Representatives of many Indian tribes had already arrived at Vincennes when Putnam and Heckeweller arrived at the post on September 12, 1792. The Wabash tribes included the Weas and the Piankashaws. Other tribes at the fort were Kaskaskias, Peorias, Musquitons, Kickapoos, Mascoutens and the Potawatomis. Putnam recorded that about 686 Indians, including men, women and children, had assembled at Vincennes. The Potawatomis that attended were a branch of the tribe located along the Illinois River in current Illinois. The eastern branch of the tribe, located in the

St. Joseph River region of current Northwestern Indiana, had denounced thier kinsmen for attending the conference.

Mr. Vandeburgh took Heckeweller to his home where he attended his needs during his illness. It would be a month before Heckeweller recovered from the fever.

September 13, 1792 - Putnam Releases Indian Prisoners to their Tribes

When the assembled Indians saw the prisoners that the Putnam party had brought along to Vincennes, they were jubilant. Putnam released them the next day, on September 13, which led to a great celebration. The natives fired guns into the air and there was much dancing and singing.

September 19, 1792 - Drovers Arrive With Cattle

Drovers from Kentucky arrived at Vincennes with a herd of 110 cattle that would serve as food for the garrison of Fort Knox and the treaty attendees.

September 20, 1792 - Heckeweller Tours Vincennes

Heckeweller recorded in his journal that more Indians arrived daily, bringing the number up close to 700 assembled natives on the outskirts of Vincennes. Putnam had to forbid the Americans from giving them whiskey, as their drinking caused many problems. On September 19, Heckeweller rode out into the countryside to tour the country with several other gentlemen. The town had been established in 1732 near the intersection of the Buffalo Trace and the Wabash River. By 1770 the town had grown to include 300 houses and contained some 1500 inhabitants, mostly French from Canada. Heckeweller noted that during that time the French inhabitants had refused to pay the priest at the church, who departed. At this time, the French Catholic inhabitants travel 300 miles by water periodically to take communion. These French were mostly fur traders and The British had taken possession of the town by virtue of the peace treaty that ended the French and Indian War in 1763. The British held it until George Rogers Clark and his small band of soldiers took the town, first in 1778, and again in February 1779 after the British recaptured the town.

Growing American Presence

After the Revolution, Americans from southern areas of the United States began filtering into Vincennes. An Indian village inhabited by members of the Wawiachtenos tribe had been located on the outskirts of Vincennes for almost fifty years. After the arrival of the "Virginians," as the Indians called all Americans, trouble started. Because of a number of incidents and murders, the village had moved some distance away. A group of these "Virginians," had gathered together and massacred these Indians, creating a great deal of trouble for the French inhabitants of Vincennes.

French Refused to Farm

The Indians refused to come to Vincennes to trade their furs, causing the French fur traders to fall into poverty. Not knowing how to farm, they refused to learn, instead relying on help from the American government to survive. He noted that the French still adopted Indian dress did not tend their gardens and that their cattle were starving. He reports that their homes are mostly one story homes with massive beams supporting the roofs. They had chimneys constructed from mortar and wood. Since stone around Vincennes was scarce and expensive, he saw no stone buildings, only ones constructed of wood. He observed fine meadows on the outskirts of town that would produce plenty of hay for the cattle; however the traders did not make use of them. Heckeweller had heard that a few miles west of Vincennes another settlement along the White River had been made that contained the "Virginians," as well as the French that could farm. Meadows many miles long lined the river on which buffalo grazed. The Indians spent the autumn hunting these animals for food and their fur.

Sugarloaf Hills

Heckeweller noted the presence of several "sugarloaf" hills near Vincennes. A trek to the top of these hills allows the observer a commanding view of Vincennes and the surrounding countryside.

The Countryside

Heckeweller noted that the Wabash River's water was clear and produced an abundance of fish and was navigable for several hundred miles from its mouth on the Ohio River. The soil was black and fertile.

September 24, 1792 - Negotiations Begin Treaty of Vincennes

A delegation of Indians had approached General Putnam on September 23, begging him to begin the negotiations, as the season advanced and they wished to begin their fall hunt. Putnam had agreed and told them that he would begin the talks at 10:00 AM, with a cannon firing as a signal. At 10:00 Putnam had the cannon fired and the talks began with a speech by the general indicating to all the assembled tribes that the United States wished to live in peace with the Indians and would give them a chance to talk about their issues until they had all been cleared away. After his speech, the talks adjourned until the following day.

September 27, 1792 - Treaty of Vincennes Signed

The negotiations went on for four days, during which the Indians professed that they believed that the whites should stay south of the Ohio River. They also maintained that the two peoples should not live together because bad people on both sides made trouble. At length, the Indians and the Putnam delegation came to an agreement and signed a treaty on September 27, 1792. The treaty contained the following five articles:

1: There would always be peace between the United States and the tribes of the Wabash and Illinois

2: The chiefs that signed the agreement agreed that they and their tribes were under the protection of the United States

3: The tribes would release all white or Negro prisoners that they held

4: The United States guaranteed that all lands to which the Indians had just claim were theirs and that none of these lands should take from them except by fair purchase. All the lands belonged originally to the Indians and they had a right to sell, or refuse to sell, these lands. The treaty guaranteed that the United States would protect these rights.

5: The Indians promised that they would stop attacking white settlements and abducting people and horses

6: If attacks did occur, reprisal was forbidden until the parties responsible have either satisfied the demand for satisfaction or refused

7. All animosities of the past were over and that both the United States and the various Indian tribes would faithfully execute the treaty.

When the parties signed the treaty, they fired a cannon eight times in celebration, with General Putnam firing the first shot, followed by seven of the chiefs. Putnam issued the

Indians four large steers, food and brandy to hold a celebration. The Indians proceeded to get drunk. Four of them fell down and died as a result of their injuries.

September 28, 1792 - Putnam Becomes Sick With Fever

General Putnam had been sick for a week, however on September his condition worsened and he had to stay in bed. His condition became such that his companions feared he would die. The same fever that afflicted both Heckeweller and Putnam had afflicted several of the people around Vincennes and some had died of it.

September 29, 1792 - Indians Stage Celebration

To celebrate the signing of the treaty, the various Indian nations gathered at Vincennes decided to stage a celebration. They tried to make themselves as hideous as possible. The members of each tribe painted themselves differently, disfigured their faces, wore green garlands around their necks and put dried deer feet on their legs that rattled when they moved. They formed a parade that moved through the streets of Vincennes, beating their drums and singing while they carried their weapons. After parading almost naked through the streets, they retired to the Vincennes city hall where they danced and regaled each other with stories of war.

September 30, 1792 - Gifts Distributed to the Indians

Gifts to the Indians were an important part of the negotiating process. The most common presents included clothing, blankets, fabrics, ammunition, weapons and medals. Cast in Philadelphia, the medals varied in size. Putnam would have given the biggest medals to the most important of the chiefs attending the negotiations. The distribution of the gifts went on for several days.

September 30, 1792 - Grand Council at the mouth of the Auglaize River

On September 30, 1792 tribes belonging to the Northwest Indian Confederacy met at a village called Au Glaize and would remain in conference until October 9, when it disbanded.

Au Glaize

Located at the confluence of the Auglaize and Maumee Rivers, the site is now the city of Defiance, Ohio. The tribes that made up the Confederacy chose this site as their headquarters during this Council. It was centrally located between many of the principal villages of the tribe, Detroit to the north and Fort Jefferson to the south. The site was composed of a French trading post, an English trading post and seven villages near the site. The Maumee River was also am important trade route during the period. The important village of Kekionga was about forty miles to the east, near the portage trail that led to the Wabash River. Thus, the Maumee formed an important trading link in a chain that stretched from Lake Erie to the mouth of the Mississippi River at New Orleans.

Northwest Indian Confederacy

The tribes had formed the Confederacy in 1783 at Detroit. The tribal members included the Shawnee, Delaware, Wyandot, Miami, Munsee, Nanticoke, Connoy, Mahigan, Ottawa, Potawatomi, Chippewa, Cherokee, Creek, Sauk, Quiatenon, Fox, the Seven Nations of Lower Canada, and Six Nations. The river's mouth is in current northwest Ohio about 45 miles from Fort Wayne, Indiana near the town of Defiance, Ohio. The confederacy had no absolute ruler and all parties in the Confederacy had an equal voice. The various tribes had to reach a consensus before a decision could be made.

The Conflict Between the Americans and the Tribes

It its inception in 1783 the tribal members agreed that the 1768 Treaty of Fort Stanwix had established the Ohio River as the boundary between the United States and the Indian nations. The natives realized that the 1783 Treaty of Paris signed between the United States and Great Britain that granted the United States independence had ignored the needs of the native tribes that occupied the vast region north of the Ohio River. They also guessed that the United States had no intention of adhering to a treaty agreed to between Great Britain and the various tribes before the nation gained independence. The United States had taken advantage of the loose nature of the Confederacy by signing several treaties with individual tribes, which had not been approved by the other tribes in the Confederacy. The other members of the Confederacy did not recognize any of these treaties.

The Council

The meeting's purpose was to decide what to do in the situation with the United States. The tribes that belonged to this loose confederacy attended this council. British agent Alexander McKee also attended the meeting and kept minutes of the affair. Many of the tribes felt that they should sue for peace with the Americans while they had the advantage. The tribes had dealt the Americans two decisive defeats and felt they were in the stronger position and asserted that they should continue the war and destroy all of the forts north of the Ohio River. The consensus the tribes arrived at involved attacking the American forts sometime around the anniversary of the date of the Battle of the Wabash. The tribes also made arrangement to meet the

Americans sometime in the spring of 1793. The meeting continued until around October 9.

Alexander McKee (1738 - January 05, 1799)

The son of Thomas McKee and a white woman named Mary, a captive of the Shawnee from a North Carolina. He was native to McKees Half Falls, Cumberland, Pennsylvania. Mary died while McKee was quite young, after which his father married a woman named Margaret Tecumsapah Opessa. Margaret was an aunt to Tecumseh, who would rise to become a great chief later in this chronicle. His father educated him to become a trader, like himself, while his stepmother taught him the ways of the Shawnee. This education from his father and stepmother served him well, as he became a successful trader and maintained a good relationship with the Indians in the Wabash River region his entire life.

Trader

He established a trading business in McKees Rocks sometime around 1764, Pennsylvania, which is on the south bank of the Ohio River in western Pennsylvania. Here he built a large home where he hosted George Washington in 1770. He dwelt there through the beginning of the Revolutionary War. A dispute with the American caused him to migrate to Detroit where he aligned himself with the British. During these years he met, and became associated with, Simon Girty and his brothers. During the war he worked with the British to establish alliances with the Indian tribes in what would become the Northwest Territory. His actions led the United States to consider him a traitor. He married three times, to Edna Yellow Britches Edna Mckee, Rising Sun, Shawnee Kispoko. McKee had six children.

October 1792

Early October - William Smalley's Hunting Trip

William Smalley had been held captive by the Indian tribe that had adopted him many years before. His Indian father had agreed to allow him to escape after Smalley told him he had a wife and children at his settlement near Fort Washington and that he wanted to return to them. They planned to take an autumn hunting trip, during which Smalley could escape, giving Smalley's Indian father an excuse to say that Smalley escaped during the night while they slept. His Indian brother had agreed to accompany him as far as the settlement, to make sure he got back safe.

Hunting Trip in Early October

Smalley and his Indian father had gone of several short hunting trips, with the permission of the chief, during the summer. Smalley always returned, as he promised he would, to gain their trust. The Indians captured Smalley's neighbor during this period. Smalley lived in fear that the man would mention his wife and children, which would result in Smalley's death. The man did not. Thus, sometime in early October Smalley set out with his Indian brother and father on the hunting trip that would result in Smalley's return home.

Early October, 1792 - Smalley's Brother's Injury Foils their Plan

During the first night of their hunting trip, Smalley's Indian brother developed a shooting pain in his hip that shot down his leg. His leg and hip swelled up, rending him incapable of traveling. Their plans foiled, the party camped for several days as Smalley and his Indian father cared for the man.

October 05, 1792, Heckeweller Begins Journey Along Buffalo Trace

As part of the treaty negotiations, Putnam had gotten the Indians to travel to Philadelphia to visit with the President and had agreed to accompany them. Putnam prevailed upon Heckeweller to begin the journey to Pennsylvania without him, as his illness prevented him from traveling. Thus, on October 4, he sent a delegation of Indian chiefs out with peace messages, accompanied by William Wells, to the hostile Indian nations that had not attended the negotiations at Vincennes. On the 5th, Heckeweller, sixteen Indian chiefs and a squaw, two Kentucky guides, two soldiers set out under the command of a Lieutenant Prior. The company of twenty-three would travel overland along the Buffalo, or Vincennes, Trace to Fort Steuben at the Falls of the Ohio.

Buffalo Trace

The Buffalo Trace began in the prairies of Illinois as the herds of buffalo headed east toward the licks. it crossed the Wabash River near the site of Vincennes, Indiana, providing the French with an ideal spot to establish the trading post that became the city. It crossed southern Indiana, nearing the Ohio River at its shallowest point, the Falls of the Ohio. After crossing the river, the bison traveled across northern Kentucky until they reached the area of the licks. In places the Trace was up to twenty feet wide. Amerindians used the trace both to hunt the bison and travel cross country. Since it connected the Ohio, Wabash and Mississippi Rivers the trace provided a highway for the white settlers that wished to go west. Today portions of U. S. 150 follow the Trace, which is now part of the National Scenic Byways Program.

http://www.fhwa.dot.gov/byways/byways/76130

October 09, 1792 - Heckeweller Party Reaches Buffalo Salt (French) Lick

The delegation departed Fort Knox on October 5, 1792. As the party passed the fort, soldiers inside fired a salute of seven cannon shots. Their route was over the Buffalo, or Vincennes, Trace. Modern US Route 150 follows the approximate path of this trace. Heckeweller notes that they traveled through a fine, level countryside, bathed in the fragrance of ripening persimmons. By evening they crossed the White River, probability somewhere east or southeast of current Loogootee, Indiana. Here, the Kentucky hunters that had accompanied them shot seven wild turkeys, so the party ate well while they camped.

The Second Day

The party hiked along the White River for a distance of about twelve miles before branching off into the wild country. Their path made difficult by shrubs and wild grapes, their progress slowed. On this part of the trail, one of the hunters shot an old buffalo that weighed close to 800 pounds.

Third Day

Heckeweller notes that the terrain changed to a mountainous, difficult trek as they entered the steep hills of the Knobstone Escarpment in the current Hoosier National Forest. Their campsite that night was along a stream that had dried up. The next day, they reached the mineral springs of French Lick.

October 11, 1792 - Heckeweller Party Overtaken by Thunderstorm

Heckeweller noted that the area around the salt licks had an abundance of buffalo bones and skulls littered about the area. Several trails led out from the licks and, as the guides were off hunting, Heckeweller and his companions took the wrong path. They proceeded a short distance before the guides returned and directed them to the right path. After they traveled about five miles a herd of buffalo galloped towards them, which they shot into. They killed one animal, which they used for meat, and wounded another. They consumed the meat that night. Some of the Indians ate so much that the next day they were sick.

Thunderstorm

On October 12th, the party was within 18 miles of Clarksville. A fierce thunderstorm enveloped them, drenching them with torrents of water. The storm was not their only worry, as they had reached a location on the road that Miami warriors often used to travel into Kentucky to raid. The party feared the warriors less than any pursuit by vengeful whites if the Indians had conducted any recent raids. If a band of whites bent on revenge encountered Heckeweller's attendant Indians, he feared they would attack them. The storm passed and the commander of the group ordered a forced march so they would quickly leave the area of danger. They marched in pouring rain the remainder of the night, reaching Clarksville early the next morning.

October 12, 1792 - Heckeweller Party Reaches Clarksville

The Heckeweller party reached Clarksville, drenched in the pouring rain. Still three miles from Fort Steuben, the group trudged on. Upon arrival, the Indians demanded brandy, so they would not get sick from the wet and cold. The commander gave them brandy, which they imbibed until all were intoxicated. Heckeweller reprimanded him, reminding him that Congress had invited the natives to come to Philadelphia to consult and that they were the commander's responsibility. The commander at first did not relent, however when Heckeweller threatened to leave the expedition and report him to his superiors, he relented. He would give the Indians no more brandy. Heckeweller spent the next several days visiting with his friend, Captain Doyle, and visiting other friends in Louisville.

October 16, 1792 - Heckeweller Party Departs Fort Steuben

Heckweller and his party boarded canoes which had been repaired and made ready to use on October 16, 1792. Traveling upstream, they soon ran into trouble, as the boats were overloaded and the five Indian chiefs believed that they were too important and wise to have to paddle the canoe. They sat in the canoes, smoking tobacco, eating and drinking. The party made slow progress. The five soldiers cursed at the chiefs, who threatened to return to the forests. Heckweller proposed to the commander that he and the guides should go ashore and travel on land and that he should instruct the men paddling the canoes that they should not approach the shore. The commander, mystified, agreed to follow Heckeweller's instructions. Thus landed, Heckeweller and his companions on shore immediately perceived a wildcat, which they shot at and missed. Shortly thereafter they shot some turkeys and a bear cub. The

Indians, seeing this, immediately ordered the oarsmen to steer towards the shore. When the men did not comply, they jumped overboard and waded ashore, saying that they should be in charge of hunting. Heckeweller and his companions thus boarded the canoes. The canoes, with less weight, traveled faster and with less danger of overturning and the problem was solved.

October 24, 1792 - Heckeweller Party Reaches Fort Washington

The remainder of the journey from Fort Steuben to Fort Washington was uneventful. The hunters killed enough game to enable the party to eat well. On October 18, they passed some Kentucky hunters who told them that they had best keep the Indians on board the canoe, as there were many Kentucky hunters in the area that would probably harm them. Eight days of paddling upstream finally brought them to Fort Washington. Upon their landing at about 1:00 PM, the soldiers in the fort shot the cannon fifteen times in their honor.

November 1792

November 03, 1792 - Little Turtle, Captures 3 Soldiers from Fort Hamilton

The Indians at the Grand Council at the mouth of the Auglaize River had agreed to launch a raid against the settlers, Little Turtle led a band of around 200 warriors south. His band penetrated to as far as Fort Hamilton. They captured 3 men from the garrison. Several soldiers mounted a pursuit, which failed to locate the warriors and their prisoners. From the prisoners Little Turtle learned of a large supply convoy had just left Fort Hamilton, bound for Fort Jefferson.

November 01, 1792 - Heckeweller Party Departs Fort Washington

Heckeweller and the party of Indians departed from Fort Washington on November 1. The voyage upstream went smoothly, except for a couple of incidents. The most serious event took place on November 4, when they met a flotilla of 16 flatboats traveling downriver.

Flotilla

The flatboats contained about 400 Kentucky soldiers, who cursed at the Indians with Heckeweller and shouted threats. Heckeweller feared that they would follow them and attack them during the night, however, they did not. During their journey upriver they met a steady stream of flatboats carrying settlers traveling downriver.

Marietta

They reached Marietta, Ohio on November 13. Heckeweller had made arrangements to await General Putnam at Marietta, so the Indians and soldiers continued on to Fort

Pitt, and then to Philadelphia. Putnam had recovered enough from his illness to begin the journey back; however he took sick again and had to delay at Fort Steuben. Rains had caused the Ohio to rise, causing travel on the river to stop, creating another delay. When the river level fell, several flotillas of flatboats, which had been waiting at Marietta for the river level to fall, continued their journey downriver taking more settlers into the Northwest Territory. Putnam rejoined finally rejoined Heckeweller on January 18.

Fort Pitt

The two men continued on without further incident, reaching Fort Pitt on February 19. The two men continued on together until they reached Carlisle, Pennsylvania. Here, Heckeweller departed on February 29 and returned to Bethlehem, his home. Putnam continued on to Philadelphia. Unfortunately, the treaty ultimately failed, as settlers continued pouring downstream and the tribes that did not sign the treaty continued their attacks, as the attack on Fort St. Clair on November 6 indicated.

November 09, 1792 - Advance Party Begins Clearing Legionville Site

As General Anthony Wayne began assembling his new Legion of the United States, he had Fort Lafayette constructed near present downtown Pittsburg in June 1792. Pittsburg, which General Wayne described as "a frontier Gomorrah," proved to be an unsatisfactory site to train his troops. The vices of Pittsburg proved too great a temptation for his fledgling Legion of the United States, so he searched for a suitable place to train his troops away from the drinking, gambling and other vices of the frontier city. His scouts located a spot on, or near, a former Indian village called Logstown, about twenty-two miles away from

Pittsburg and on the east side of the Ohio River, near the current town of Baden, Pennsylvania.

Legionville

On November 9 a construction force of about 200 soldiers arrived on the site. They began clearing the area and erecting buildings and fortifications. Surrounded by steep ravines on the east, west and north, he had the camp laid out on an east/west axis. He had four defensive redoubts, smaller forts built outside the main fort to protect soldiers outside the main fort, constructed around the fort. He also directed the soldiers to dig a defensive ditch around the fort. This ditch was more than a mile long when complete. He stationed 36 men in each redoubt and maintained an additional garrison of 120 men to guard the fort while construction was under way. By the time the main force arrived to train at the 35 acre site, Legionville contained almost 500 buildings. These included barracks, housing for Wayne and the other officers, a hospital, storage buildings, powder magazines and other structures.

November 06, 1792 - Little Turtle Attacks Fort. St. Clair

During the evening of November 5, 1792, Little Turtle's band of warriors had located the supply convoy camped outside Fort St. Clair that was traveling to carry supplies to Fort Jefferson.

Attack

The Indians attacked at daybreak, just as the commander of the convoy, John 'Adair, began recalling the sentries. The Indians breached the camp, forcing many of the soldiers to fight hand to hand. Adair managed to lead his men in an orderly retreat to a stockade outside the walls, where they made a stand about eighty yards from the site the fight began. At some point in the action they were re-supplied with ammunition from inside the fort. The fight continued as the soldiers forced the warriors to retreat though the camp, when the Indians turned and made a stand about 600 yards from where the battle began. They once again forced the soldiers to retreat, which they did while cursing the enemy.

Successful Stand

Once again the soldiers stood and eventually forced the Indians to retreat just as the soldiers began running out of ammunition. Finally, the Indians broke and ran. Adair had his men pursue the force a short distance; however he called off the pursuit due to the shortage of ammunition.

Interred

Six soldiers died in the battle and another four wounded. Four were missing in action. Native losses are unknown. The soldiers are interred near the former fort's site, Fort St. Clair Park. The graveyard is about fifty paces north, beneath the "Whispering Oak", which still stands and is over 200 years old. Established in 1923, the park finds use as a Santa Land with extensive light and decoration displays at Christmas time. Visitors can find the fort outside Eaton Ohio, though only a few remnants of the fort remain. The nearby Fort Saint Clair Museum maintains some historical exhibits about the fort and Preble County.

Fort St. Clair Park

135 Camden Rd

Eaton, Ohio.

November 28, 1792 - General Wayne's Troops Arrive at Legionville

General Anthony Wayne arrived at Legionville with his troops on November 28, 1794. Wayne had the soldiers begin the task of building permanent quarters. The weather was turning colder with winter's approach and the men needed better living quarters than the linen tents they occupied upon arrival. The general course of action was to build the commanding officer's quarters first, followed by officer's quarters and then the barracks that housed the soldiers. General Wayne reversed this procedure, having the soldiers build their own barracks first, followed by the officer's quarters and then his own. The soldiers occupied themselves for the first weeks building housing for themselves and the officers, using the ample supplies of trees as construction materials.

December 1792

December 30, 1792 - Approximate Date of William Smalley's Return

Smalley and his Indian father had managed to get Smalley's Indian brother to a French trader's cabin that was along the shores of Lake Erie. Smalley's Indian father spoke to the trader, telling him that Smalley had been kidnapped and wanted to return home. The Frenchman told him he did not dare to help Smalley, but that there was an extra canoe by the shore. If Smalley took the canoe one night while everyone slept, he could make his getaway. When pressed about payment, the Frenchman said he needed an ox yoke. If Smalley could make him an ox yoke, he would consider it payment for the canoe. Smalley agreed and made the yoke. A couple of nights later, Smalley took the canoe and paddled along the lake to Presque Isle, now Erie, Pennsylvania. He made his way through the forests to the Allegheny River. He traveled down the Allegheny to its junction with the Ohio River and thence to Columbia, where he was reunited with his friends and family sometime in late December, 1792.

Early December 1792 - Wayne's Army Completes Building Living Quarters - Training Resumes

By early December the troops had finished constructing the buildings that would comprise Legionville. The structures, about 500 in all, included single story cabins for the various troops and two story cabins for the officers. The hospital and General Wayne's quarters were two story cabins with chimneys on both ends.

The Training

Secretary of War Henry Knox's instructions to General Wayne had been blunt, "another conflict with raw recruits is to be avoided at all means." Wayne distributed copies of

General Baron von Steuben's military manual to the troops and began a rigorous training routine. Wayne also instituted a new method of firing at the enemy. Previously, American troops fired in volleys aimed in the general direction of the natives using a single lead ball loaded in the gun. The muskets then used were not generally known for accuracy, thus this type of fire was effective with massed armies. However, the Indians did not fight in a mass; they attacked randomly and fired only after aiming directly at a foe.

New Method

Wayne trained his soldiers in a new method of firing called "buck and ball." This load included a .50- .75 caliber round ball along with up to a half dozen smaller lead pellets. This load ensured a greater degree of probability that the shot would at least inflict some damage on the enemy. He also trained his soldiers in marksmanship, rewarding the better sharpshooters with an extra ration of rum. The aimed-fire method of shooting would, Wayne hoped, give his soldiers much better success than the troops led by Harmar and St. Clair. General Wayne also considered the bayonet a useful weapon against native warriors, as they did not have them. He trained them well in its use and its ability to break up Indian battle formations.

Native Tactics and Weaponry

A word about the weaponry and battle tactics of the native warriors the Legion would face is necessary. Amerindian warriors used a variety of weapons when fighting against the Americans. These weapons included the traditional bow and arrow, clubs, tomahawks and knives. The British outposts like Detroit supplied them with guns. The natives favored a gun called the "Brown Bess," which was a .75 caliber muzzle loading weapon officially designated as the British Land Pattern musket. As marksmen the Amerindian warrior tended to be an exceptionally good. The necessity of hunting fast moving game required the development of this skill, which they used quite effectively against American soldiers. They were also skilled at loading the muskets quickly. One survivor of the Battle of the Wabash (Battle of the Pumpkin Fields) reported that he witnessed one warrior run for a tree, and upon reaching it, fire and load four times before the soldier could bring his musket to bear. He noted that the native hit his target with every shot. The warrior loaded his musket using a variety of projectiles, the most common being one large shot and several smaller ones. For close in hand to hand fighting the warrior used the knife, tomahawk and war club.

Battle Tactics

Amerindian tactics featured a quick, fierce attack. Native strategy required good cover, like trees, bushes, logs and other natural features. They excelled at ambushes and raids, striking quickly and aggressively. The natives had developed an extensive system of narrow trails that snaked through the forests over the centuries. Used mainly for trade and migration between summer and winter camps, warriors used these trails to move great distances quickly through the forests to attack, and them melt silently back into the forest. Natives typically organized themselves into small bands of about twenty warriors. Usually composed of fighters from the same tribe, four of these warriors took the responsibility of hunting game for the remainder of the band. These small bands could move quickly, sustaining themselves from the game they killed during their operation. The tactics, speed of attack, master of weaponry and ability to move quickly through the dense forest made the Indians of the Northwest Indian Confederacy a formidable foe.

Baron von Steuben (September 17, 1730 - November 28, 1794)

The Baron's full birth name, Friedrich Wilhelm Ludolf Gerhard Augustin von Steuben, is a bit of a mouthful, and we now know him simply as Baron Von Steuben. His birth to Royal Prussian Engineer, Capt. Baron Wilhelm von Steuben and Elizabeth von Jagvodin took place in the Prussian military fortress town of Magdeburg, Germany. He trained from early manhood as a soldier, first serving with his father as a volunteer in the War of the Austrian Succession at age fourteen. In 1747 he joined the Prussian Army and served in the Seven Years War, getting wounded at the Battle of Prague. He received another wound at the Battle of Kunersdorf in 1759 during the same war. The Russians took him prisoner at Major General von Knoblock's surrender on the eastern front. in 1762. The Russians released him in 1762, when he received a promotion to captain. This promotion eventually led to his appointment as aide-de-camp to Frederick the Great.

When the war ended in 1763, the Army reduced its forces and released Von Steuben. He found employment serving as Grand Marshall for Fürst Josef Friedrich Wilhelm of Hohenzollern-Hechingen from 1764 until 1777. It was during this time he became acquainted with French Minister of War (Count de St. Germain). During 1771 the Prince of Hollenzollern-Hechingen bestowed the title "Baron" to him, thus he now became Baron Von Steuban. He was looking for work as a soldier in 1777 when he traveled to France in 1777. French Foreign Minister Comte de Saint-Germain sensed the value that a former Prussian Army officer could have to the American cause. By now allied to America, St. Germain introduced him to Benjamin Franklin, who in turn recommended him to General George Washington via letter. Washington wrote back that the Continental Congress could promise neither pay nor rank and he would have to present himself to Congress as a volunteer.

Disgusted, he returned to Prussia to find allegations of improper relationships while in Prince Josef Friedrich Wilhelm of Hohenzollern-Hechingen's service. The allegations carried charges of homosexual conduct, never proven, and would prove disastrous for his hopes of military promotion. He returned to Paris and accepted Franklin's proposal. The French government paid his passage, and he arrived in Philadelphia in December 1, 1777. Because he had outfitted himself in a red uniform, the Americans mistook him for a British officer and almost arrested him. After Congress reviewed him and made arrangements for payment at the conclusion of the war, the Congress sent him to General Washington. General Washington received him on February 23, 1778.

Inspector General

The General appointed Von Steuben Inspector General with the task of write standard drills for an army that used different training methods from company to company. Since he could not write English, he wrote his orders in the military language of Europe, French. Washington's aides-de-camps, John Laurens and Alexander Hamilton, translated the orders into English. Brigade inspectors then copied the lessons into the orderly book for each brigade and regiment. He also instituted a change in the layout of the camps. Before his arrival the soldiers relieved themselves anywhere they wished. They killed animals for consumption in the middle of the camp and left the remains in place. He reorganized the entire camp, placing the latrines on the lower end and the kitchens on the upper end of the camp. Baron Von Steuben transformed the Continental Army from a rag tag fighting force into a well drilled, professional army.

Steuben's Military Training Program

Using the skills he learned in the best military in the world, the Prussian Army, he upgraded the training drills practiced by the soldiers under Washington's command. He hand picked 120 soldiers and used them as incubators for his training methods. Because he used profanity in several languages profusely and worked directly with the soldiers, they loved him and with eagerness learned his methods. They, in turn, went out and trained the other soldiers.

The Congress, due to lack of funds, could never pay him what it promised. New York, Pennsylvania, and Virginia each granted him lands. He sold portions of these lands, finally retiring to some holdings in New York, where he died in 1794.

March 1793

Early March, 1793 - Indian Chiefs Visit Legionville to Discuss Terms for Peace

The United States had concerns about the state of affairs with the members of the Iroquois League, who seemed well disposed towards the United States. In spite of this, the Iroquois League nations were restless and nervous over the developing situation. To temper the situation, General Anthony Wayne invited several of the chiefs to visit Legionville. In early March several of the chiefs, including Cornplanter, Big Tree, Guasutha and New Arrow visited the camp to discuss peace. The native chiefs appeared impressed with the order and discipline General Wayne's troops possessed, in contrast with the largely undisciplined troops that had previously gone to war with the Wabash tribes.

No Negotiating

The chiefs maintained that as long as settlers insisted upon settling north of the Ohio River, there could be no peace. The Wabash tribes had just won two major conflicts with the United States and were in no mood to negotiate. At this point, the United States had sent several expeditions into the Wabash Region seeking to negotiate. The expeditions headed by Antoine and Pierre Gamelin from Vincennes in 1790 had failed. Thomas Proctor, in his 1791 expedition, had gotten no further than Buffalo Creek on the shore of Lake Erie before turning back because of threats of death if he went any further. During the previous year, 1792, the United States had sent Major Alexander Trueman and Isaac Freeman to Kekionga to negotiate. The missions had ended in the murder of the negotiators. General Rufus Putnam and John Heckeweller had gotten a treaty of sorts signed at Vincennes, however even that effort seemed to have been for naught. As March drew to a close, Wayne began preparing his troops for the journey down the Ohio and to war.

April 1793

April 30, 1793 - Legion of the United States Departs Legionville

By April 30, 1993 General Anthony Wayne believed that his troops were ready, so he gave the order to ready them for departure.

Difficult Winter

The winter spent at Legionville had turned the raw recruits into well trained soldiers. The experience had not been without costs as young men penned up in close quarters led to disciplinary problems, personal conflicts and other problems. Wayne was a strict disciplinarian who imposed harsh punishments for even minor infractions. Drunkenness led to dismissal. Other infractions could lead to branding on the forehead, lashes or even death. Duels were also a problem, as personal disagreements could lead to the antagonists fighting a duel to settle their differences. At least three men died during the encampment, the result of fifteen duels.

Departure

General Wayne had assembled the largest single flotilla, over thirty barges, to float down the Ohio River. The barges, each flying their unit's flag, kept a distance of about 100 yards from each other as they traveled downstream on the flooded Ohio River's vigorous current at twice the usual speed. The Legion arrived at Fort Washington in early May.

May 1793

May 05, 1793 - Legion of the United States Arrives at Fort Washington

Major General Anthony Wayne and his flotilla of barges arrived at Fort Washington on May 5, 1793, with great fanfare from the local citizens. To avoid the alcohol and other temptation a wild, frontier community offered lonely soldiers; Wayne ordered that the army set up camp a few miles southwest of Fort Washington at the farm of Thomas Hobson. Using a play of words on the man's name, Wayne dubbed the fort Hobson's Choice, a phrase defined by Webster as being "...the necessity of accepting one of two or more equally objectionable alternatives." The camp was located near the mouth of Mill Creek, on the Ohio River. Despite the distance between the camp and Cincinnati, Wayne still had problems keeping his soldiers sober.

Early May 1793 - Wabash Tribes Gather for Council

The Wabash tribes had signaled a desire to meet with the Americans in the spring of 1793 to discuss further the worsening situation in the lands north of the Ohio River. The natives were in discord over how they should handle the gathering threat of the increasing numbers of settlements in the region, thus the council was delayed. The tribes decided they needed to gather in council among themselves to decide what they should tell the American commissioners when they arrived at the council. Sometime in early May, the tribes began to assemble for this council.

Mid May, 1793 - Joseph Brandt Meets with John Graves Simcoe

In a bid to help negotiate a peace, Mohawk leader Joseph Brandt began making preparations to travel to the meeting place between the natives and the Americans. On the way, he stopped to discuss the situation with British Lieutenant Governor John Graves Simcoe at Niagra on the Lake in Upper Canada (Ontario).

John Graves Simcoe (February 25, 1752 – October 26, 1806)

The son of John and Katherine Simcoe, John was native to Cotterstock, Oundle, England. His father, a British navy officer, died of pneumonia when he was seven. His three siblings also died while they were young, thus John was the only surviving son of the Simcoe's. He recieved his education at Exeter Grammar School and Eton College, and spent some time studying at Merton College, Oxford. He gained his law license after admittance at Lincoln's Inn; however he decided to enter the British Army in 1770 to follow the wishes of his father.

Revolutionary War

Simcoe's assignment as an ensign serving in the 35th Regiment of Foot found him deployed to Boston in April, 1775 at the start of the American Revolution. He received promotion to captain during the siege. Simcoe saw extensive action during the war, receiving a wound at the September 11, 1777 Battle of Brandywine. He led his unit; the Queen's Rangers, at the Battle of Crooked Billet and led an action called Simcoe's Raid in October 1779. He was captured during this raid, but was released later that year. Simcoe continued serving during the war and was at the Siege of Yorktown.

Back to England

The Army invalided him back to England after the war. In 1790 he entered politics and gained election to Parliament. He received appointment as lieutenant governor of the new loyalist province of Upper Canada on September 12, 1791. Delays due to weather kept him from arriving at his post in Kingston, Upper Canada until June 24, 1792. Simcoe was committed to the British policy of maintaining an Indian nation in the area north of the Ohio River in order to make it a buffer state between the United States and British Canada

The Meeting

Simcoe had received a set of 1786 maps drawn up by British Governor at the time Sir William Johnson. The maps provided strong evidence that the boundary between the Indian tribes and the American settlements in Kentucky to be the Ohio River. Brandt studied the maps, and took them, hoping they would provide the Indian tribes with some strong ammunition in the coming council at Sandusky. Brandt had become convinced that the Indians would ultimately lose any war between the united tribes and that peace was the only way to preserve the Indian way of life.

May 24, 1793 - Wayne Sends Reinforcements to Fort Jefferson

Major General Anthony Wayne sent a company of 100 riflemen north to Fort Jefferson to reinforce that important post. Wayne also issued orders to widen the road that led from Fort Washington to Fort Hamilton.

June 1793

June 06, 1793 - Indian Attacks Near Fort Hamilton

In attacks spreading over multiple days from June 5 through the 17th attacks by native warriors killed seven people. The natives also stole a number of horses and wounded several people at these incidents near Forts Hamilton and Randolph.

June 1793 - William Henry Harrison Appointed Aide-De-Camp to General Wayne

Sometime in June 1793 General Anthony Wayne appointed William Henry Harrison, who had received promotion to lieutenant in early September 1792, retroactive to June 2, 1792.

Aide-De-Camp

The Aide-De-Camp provided a valuable service for a commanding general. Their varied duties included discussing topics with the General, then drafting a letter concerning it. After completing the draft, Wayne would make revisions and corrections and then the aide would complete the final draft and have the general sign it. He then made a copy for the "letter book." He would also make a copy of any reply to the general's letter for the letter book. If the recipient was a high ranking officer or the letter extremely important the aide would hand deliver the communication. This duty could be quite dangerous in times of battle, with many aides receiving wounds while completing their duties. The men wrote with quill pen and on parchment, methodically dipping into the ink pot as they wrote. Their duties required them to rise early in the morning and work late into the night. Harrison would serve as Wayne's Aide-De-Camp throughout the Fallen Timbers campaign. His position gave him a unique insight into

General Wayne's methods and the lessons learned served him well later in life.

Pay

Harrison received a salary of $64 per month, which was what a major received. He also had a $12 per month forage pay, which allowed him to purchase feed for the two horses he needed to carry out his duties. Harrison frequently carried dispatches between General Wilkinson, his former commanding officer, and General Wayne. A feud had developed between the two generals, a state of affairs Harrison managed to avoid being drawn into.

July 1793

July 07, 1793 - Indian Delegation Meets with Commissioners

A deputation of fifty Indian chiefs from the nations meeting at Sandusky arrived at Niagara-On-The-Lake on July 7.

The Indians Fears and Positions

Their purpose was to solidify their demand that the boundary between the Indian nations and the Americans had to be the Ohio River and that they would accept no American settlements north of the river. They questioned whether the commissioners had the authority to set the boundary at the Ohio River, as the assembled nations desired. They also expressed concern over the force that General Wayne had assembled in Indian Territory and the road he was building into the heart of their territory. Joseph Brandt acted as the mediator and translator during the council. The chiefs related that the following tribes had assembled at Sandusky and were in conference:

Mohawk

Onondaga

Oneida

Cayuga

Seneca

Wyandotte

Shawnee

Delaware

Muncie

Miami

Ottawa

Chippewa

Potawatami

Mingo

Cherokee

Creek

Nantikokes

The representatives of the tribes made clear that the numbers and tribes changed daily as new representatives arrived.

The Commissioners Position

Benjamin Lincoln, speaking for the commissioners, expressed his regrets that the United States had felt it necessary to assemble a military force and the President Washington had forbidden Wayne to take up hostilities against the natives unless they were attacked first. Secondly, they made it known that they did have the authority to set the boundary, however they were sure that both parties would have to make compromises about the boundary during the negotiations.

Confusion

During the discussions Brandt had given the impression to the Americans that the natives were willing to make compromises on the settlements already in existence and the border. The meetings would go on for three days, after which the natives agreed to accompany the commissioners to Sandusky to continue the talks.

July 10, 1793 - William Wells Reaches Indian Council

William Wells had traveled to Vincennes with Rufus Putnam and John Heckeweller to act as an interpreter during the negotiations. The Shawnee and the Delaware had not signed the treaty and did not want peace. Sometime in June or July 1793 Wells had volunteered to travel to an Indian council being held at the rapids of the Miami River, near the current city of Toledo Ohio, and gather intelligence about the state of the Indian tribes. He arrived at the council on July 10 to find that about 1500 natives had assembled for the council. That number would swell to around 2000 in a few days, the vast majority of which were warriors eager for war.

Late July 1793 - Brandt Meets With Indians at Sandusky

The Indian delegation departed Niagara-On-The-Lake soon after the conference and returned to Sandusky to confer with the tribes gathered there. Brandt joined them at Sandusky and tried to convince them to accept an alternate border other than the Ohio. The natives refused. British agent Alexander McKee had joined the assemblage and told the chiefs that the British would supply them with arms and ammunition if they resisted. The Creek and Cherokee delegation that had arrived from the south urged the assembled Wabash tribes not to accept any compromise. The chiefs sent a message to the commissioners demanding that the Ohio River would be the border between the Americans and the Wabash tribes. Thus, the conference was in confusion over what course of action the natives should take. Meanwhile, at Hobson's Choice, General Wayne continued training his army.

July 21, 1793 - Commissioners Reach Mouth of Detroit River

Contrary winds and stalling from Governor Simcoe delayed the commissioners, forcing them to stay at Niagara-on-the-Lake until mid July. The commissioners finally set sail on the schooner *Dunmore* from Fort Erie, where they had gathered in anticipation of their journey into Indian country, sometime after July 14. They arrived at Detroit, where British Indian Agent Captain Matthew Elliot hosted them at his home. The commissioners elected to stay at Detroit until they received word that the natives were ready to meet with them at Sandusky, on the shores of Lake Erie.

Deputation of Indians

The deputation of about twenty Indians sent from the council at Sandusky arrived at Detroit sometime after the commissioners arrived. The two parties agreed to meet on July 30 in Detroit.

July 31, 1793 - Grand Council Meets with United States Commissioners

During late July 1793 the Iroquois, United States Commissioners and representatives of the Shawnee, Miami, Delaware and other tribes inhabiting the Wabash Valley met at Detroit.

The Indian's Position

The Shawnee and Miami, led by Simon Girty, insisted that the United States recognize the Treaty of Fort Stanwix, signed in 1768, that set the border between the United States and the Indian nations at the Ohio River. They also maintained that the United States must remove all forts and settlements north of the Ohio River. They repeated their demand that the United States adhere to the Treaty of Fort Stanwix and recognize the Ohio River as the boundary.

The United States Concedes

The commissioners conceded that the United States had not acquired the ownership of the lands north of the Ohio River when they signed the peace treaty with Great Britain at the end of the Revolutionary War. The Indian nations had retained the rights to the land under the 1783 Treaty of Paris. In that Treaty the King had merely transferred the right to negotiate the purchase of lands from himself to the United States. This was an important point, as during the previous eleven years the United States had claimed that the British had transferred ownership of the land to the United States.

The Commissioner's Offer

The Commissioners pointed out that in the ensuing years, settlements north of the Ohio had been established and that these settlements represented a huge investment in time, money and physical effort. They maintained that it would be impractical and too expensive to remove them. The commissioners proposed to offer the Indians a large amount of money for the lands around Fort Washington and Clark's Grant in what is now the State of Indiana. They proposed to establish a new boundary line that would establish the Indian nations as owning the lands they now occupied, but left the new settlements in place.

The Indians Retire to Sandusky

The Indian representatives that had met with the commissioners at Detroit considered the American's offer. They stated that the commissioners should not travel to Sandusky at this time, but remain in Detroit while the Indian nations considered the United State's offer. Thus, the Indian representatives returned to Sandusky and the commissioners remained at Detroit as a guest of Matthew Elliot. During the days of the council William Wells circulated through the various Indian camps at Sandusky gathering intelligence for General Wayne.

August 1793

August 13, 1793 - Indian Council Sends Declaration to United States Commissioners

The tribal leaders meeting in council at the Sandusky River council had united in their refusal to consider allowing the American settlements to stay north of the Ohio River. The tribes were disunited in their response to the threat. After further discussions, the tribal leaders sent a reply back to the American commissioners at Detroit. The chiefs refused the offer of money for their lands, as they had no use for money; however the lands in question were vital to the Indian's survival. Their reply stated, "Money, to us, is of no value, & to most of us unknown, and as no consideration whatever can induce us to sell the lands on which we get sustenance for our women and children; we hope we may be allowed to point out a mode by which your settlers may be easily removed, and peace thereby obtained. We want Peace; Restore to us our Country and we shall be Enemies no longer."

Talks Collapse

After receiving this reply, the commissioners realized that further talks were useless. They boarded their boats and sailed back home.

August 25, 1793 - General Wayne Issues Marching Orders

At Hobson's Choice General Wayne learned of the collapse of the negotiations at Detroit and began making final preparations for the march north. On August 25 he issued three important documents, the Order of March, the Order of Camp and the Order of Battle. The Order of March outlined the positions of each battalion and company of soldiers while marching. It defined the positions of the different classes of artillery, the positioning of the advance, rear and flanking guards and the disposition of the different classes of troops. It also defined the position of the contractor wagons that held the supplies, the pack horses and cattle. The Order of Battle detailed the maneuvers of the troops if engaged with the enemy. It defined the movements and maneuvers of the riflemen, cavalry, artillery and other classes of troops if engaged by the enemy. The Order of Camp defined the positions of companies, supply wagons, pack horses and guards while the army was in camp. During the remainder of the time at Hobson's choice Wayne would enforce strict discipline on the troops and drill them incessantly in the maneuvers outlined in the Orders of Battle and March. He would have his troops prepared for battle it came to that.

September 16, 1793 - William Wells Delivers Report to General Wayne

William Wells returned from his mission to gather intelligence about the state of the natives at the council. His extensive report included the following points:

The tribes demanded that the Ohio River serve as the boundary between the Indian nations and the United States

They believed that the United States should compensate them for their lost hunting lands in Kentucky

British Lieutenant Governor John Graves Simcoe's aide-de-camp and two other British officers had been at the council in company with Simon Girty and Alexander McKee

The Indian chiefs in attendance had attended a private meeting every night with the British officers

The British had supplied many arms, ammunition, gunpowder and other supplies to the natives

The British had promised as much support as the natives needed to make war upon the United States

A majority of the Indians had been inclined at least thrice to concede to allow the settlements to stay and establish a new boundary; however the British had dissuaded them

The southern tribes in attendance, the Creeks and Cherokee, supported war

The Spanish, in possession of Florida and the southern parts of current Alabama, Louisiana and Mississippi, encouraged the Creeks and Cherokee to wage war on the United States

The southern Indian tribes and the tribes of the Wabash River Valley had formed a loose confederacy and would wage a general war against the United States

The northern tribes would attack and destroy the American settlements north of the Ohio, meet at the Falls of the Ohio and invade Kentucky

They could provision themselves from Kentucky, as the Long Knives in Kentucky that lived there had plenty of corn and cattle that the warriors could use

The British promised the chiefs that they would supply them with everything they needed, provided they came to Detroit for it as the British would not bring it to them

A deserter from Wayne's army had traveled to the council and gave what intelligence he was capable of giving to the Indians in council

Indian spies were in constant view of Wayne's forces and carried frequent intelligence reports back to the Indians in council

The total number of warriors currently committed to wage war against the United States included:

Shawnees 300

Chippewa's 160

Delaware 350

part of the Six Nations 35

Miami's 100

Cherokees & other Indians living on the Miami 65

Wyandotte 200

Ottawa] 150

Pottawatomie 100

Munsees 30

There are six or seven other nations living on Lake Michigan who will - be with them say 40

Total - about 1520

Wells warned that if General Wayne delayed action, the Indians would gather at least 500 more

Their strategy was to kill the pack horses carrying supplies to the troops and then to prevent the soldiers from sleeping by keeping a constant fire on the forts every night

If the Indians believed they had sufficient numbers, they would attack immediately

Wells believed that if Wayne's forces penetrated to as far as the rapids of the river, the British would move against them

British and French militia forces that would join the Indians totaled about 1500

Wells had seen a paper that indicated that the Creeks and Cherokees had destroyed several American settlements that had become established in their regions

The Indians believed that the American army would have to divide itself to deal with the dual threats to the south and north of the Ohio

The Kentuckians would not help Wayne's forces because the incursion into their territory would keep them occupied

the Spaniards had promised the Creeks and Cherokees all the supplies and weapons they would need to wage war

After delivering the report, Wayne hired Wells to act as guide and interpreter.

October 1793

October 07, 1793 - Wayne Begins March North

After being delayed by a severe influenza epidemic that engulfed the camp, on a clear, delectable autumn day, General Anthony Wayne began his march north.

Influenza Epidemic

The influenza epidemic started in late September after Wayne had completed preparations needed to begin the march north. The symptoms included fever, vomiting, body aches and chills. Most of the troops, including General Wayne, were afflicted by the disease. The illness delayed the beginning of he March for a few days, however on October 7, 1793 General Anthony Wayne gave the order for the march to begin on the wide road he had ordered built to Fort Hamilton.

Beginning the March

Wayne estimated that his force totaled about 2600 regular troops buttressed with 360 volunteers. A company of scouts departed first, their pattern marking an arc that formed a blunt spearhead at the front of the army. Behind the scouts followed General Wayne, leading the force, with his aid-de-camp William Henry Harrison and his adjutant Edward Butler beside him. Generals Thomas Posey and James Wilkinson rode right behind him. Wayne used the marching order he had designed. The disposition of the troops ensured that every man in the moving chain of soldiers protected another man. The troops formed two columns, each marching on opposite sides of the road. The columns protected the artillery and the supply wagons, which moved down the center of the road. The supplies included a long line of pack horses carrying supplies, heavily laden wagons and the herds of cattle needed to sustain the force. Behind the supplies came the women that Wayne had allowed to accompany the army if they left their children behind at the fort. Dragoons rode on the flanks and at far in advance of the army, always searching for natives warriors waiting to attack. Riflemen and light cavalry road alongside the columns, ready to attack any enemy that tried to ambush the force. By the end of the day, the force had reached Five Mile Spring, southeast of the modern town of Five Mile. Wayne ordered that temporary breastworks and abatis to protect the slumbering army at night.

October 08, 1793 - Wayne's Forces Reach Fort Hamilton

Wayne's forces moved quickly along the wide road he had prepared. Months of packhorse activity as they moved supplies from Fort Washington and Fort Hamilton had packed the road, making it easier to travel along it. The road later became known as "Wayne's Trace."

The "Whirlwind" and the "Blacksnake"

During the campaign that came, the natives coined two nicknames for General Wayne, the "Whirlwind" and the "Blacksnake". His army moved fast, faster than any previous army through the forested frontier, earning the first name. The second he earned because of his tendency to lie in wait of his prey, like the blacksnake, waiting for the perfect moment to strike.

Short Time

Wayne's army threw up a protective embankment for protection against attack and camped for the night in the prairie near High Street in the current town of Hamilton. They remained in this camp for only one night. The next morning the army moved into heart of Indian territory.

October 13, 1793 - Wayne Camps On Greeneville Creek

Six days after departing from Hobson's Choice, General Anthony Wayne's army reached the banks of Greenville Creek at about 10:00 AM, a short distance from its junction with Mudd Creek and about sixty miles from his starting point. Wayne decided to camp at this point, as his supplies were short. St. Claire had passed over the site during his ill fated march and had noted that the site was suitable for a fort, though he constructed Fort Jefferson five miles to the south. The disastrous Battle of the Wabash had taken place about twenty miles to the northwest.

October 17, 1793 - Natives Attack Supply Wagon Convoy

A small band of Indian warriors attacked a twenty wagon supply convoy just as it crossed Seven Mile Creek a short distance north of Fort. St. Clair. The attackers killed twelve privates and one officer. There were seven men missing in action after the attack. The Indians captured the entire lead herd of seventy horses, leaving the wagons and supplies on them in the middle of the road. The loss of the horses proved troublesome some for the contractor charged with bringing supplies into the camp. Joseph Shaylor, court-martialed by General James Wilkinson, had been reinstated by General Anthony Wayne, who had placed him in command of Fort St. Clair. Shaylor had been in command of one of the columns in the convoy, on the way to Wayne's camp.

October 23, 1793 - Wayne's Report to Knox

General Anthony Wayne's report of October 23 related the aforementioned attack on the supply convoy as well as other information regarding the state of his army. This included his state of supplies, troops, intelligence gathering and future plans. The report also contained a list of casualties resulting from the attack on October 17.

Supplies

Most critical to the movement of his army was the delivery of supplies to the army. Wayne reported that the contractors responsible for moving this critical component of an army had deceived him regarding how many rations they had stocked at Fort Jefferson and their ability to move the supplies. The contractors revealed that only about one quarter of the supplies they had reported stored at Fort Jefferson were actually there. They also confessed that they only had horses and wagons enough to transport about half the rations needed to sustain the troops.

Intelligence Gathering

Wayne had enlisted William Wells and other to spread over the countryside, gathering intelligence on the state of the native forces opposing him. He learned that the Indians gathered at Au Glaize had sent the women and children home to their villages, leaving the warriors still gathered together, with more arriving at the place.

State of his Force

Wayne reported that he was camped at a site that was about halfway between Fort Jefferson and the site of St. Clair's battle on November 4, 1792. He felt confident that he could maintain his army safely at the site. He had about 70,000 rations in camp and had an additional 120,000 more in transit, if the enemy did not attack the convoy. Wayne stated that his greatest difficulty at that time was deploying a sufficient force to defend the supply convoys and leaving a satisfactory quantity of troops in camp to defend it against attack. He also expressed concern over a shortage of officers. He had three officers in custody, awaiting satisfactory conditions to conduct a court martial.

Author Note: A daily ration at this time consisted of one pound of bread or flour, one pound of beef or 3/4 pound of pork or bacon. Each 100 rations had, in addition, one quart of salt, 2 quarts of vinegar, two pounds of soap and one pound of candles.

Plans

Wayne expressed confidence he could remain in his present location and would not consider retreat, as it would embolden the enemy. As soon as his supply inventory reached a sufficient level, he proposed to advance further into enemy territory, hoping to force them to sue for peace.

The State of the Territory

At the time Wayne considered his condition at his camp on Greenville Creek, the Northwest Territory consisted of five counties, Hamilton, Knox, St. Clair, Washington and Wayne. Historians do not know the exact boundaries of this vast territory. Circuit judges traveled between the five largest towns in the Territory meting out justice. The towns were Vincennes, Marietta, Kaskaskia, Detroit and Cincinnati.

November 1793

November 21, 1793 - Wayne's Forces Begin Construction of Fort Greene

General Wayne had desired to continue marching towards the principal Indian village at the junction of the St. Mary's and St. Joseph Rivers, however it was late in the season and many of his volunteer militia objected to advancing further in the teeth of winter. Wayne had discovered a site that was located on higher ground that afforded a commanding view of the surrounding prairie lands. On the site he ordered the construction of a fortress that would become the largest wooden fort ever constructed in North America. On November 21, he ordered that construction of the new fort begin.

The Fort

When the rectangular structure was complete, it encompassed 55 acres. The palisade walls were 1800 feet long and towered ten feet over the countryside. The total length of the walls was 1.25 miles. The walls had openings for riflemen to shoot through and each of the corners had a sentry tower. At the center of each wall he had a blockhouse built. This fort became his winter headquarters and a repository for the supplies he accumulated in anticipation for the campaign which he planned for the next year. The garrison would include as many as 2000 soldiers. Wayne named the fort after his Revolutionary war compatriot and friend, Nathanial Greene.

Nathaniel Greene (August 7, 1742 - June 19, 1786)

The son of Quakers Nathaniel and Mary Mott Green, Nathanial was a native of Warwick, Rhode Island. His father was a merchant and prominent member of the Society of Friends, leading to Nathaniel's upbringing in that religion. His faith, which demanded pacifism, and his chosen career in the military led to his abandoning the faith to pursue his military talents.

Education and Early Trades

His father taught him both the blacksmith and milling trades. His formal education almost non-existent, Greene used the money he earned to buy books, which he would read diligently. He assumed the ownership of his father's forge in Coventry, Rhode Island in 1770. That same year he gained election to the Rhode Island General Assembly. He was instrumental in the formation of Coventry's first public school. During this time, he developed an interest in the military.

Marriage and Military

Greene began his military career and marriage in 1774. He married Catharine Littlefield in July 1774. Together the couple would have six children, five of whom would survive until adulthood. In August the escalating turmoil with Britain, Greene helped organize the Kentish Guards, a Rhode Island militia group. The group became officially chartered in October 1774. He began buying, and studying, books on military strategy and history about this time. Because of a limp he had since he was a boy, the leadership decreed that he could only serve as a private in the Guards. In early 1775, the disagreements between the colonists and the British erupted into gunfire. Greene traveled to Boston to help the patriot cause. George Washington, newly appointed General of the Continental Army by Congress met Greene and was impressed with his military prowess. Greene's military career as a general was about to begin.

December 1793

December 12, 1793 - Wayne Dispatches Force to Site of St. Claire's Defeat

General Anthony Wayne dispatched a force that consisted of eight infantry companies and one artillery company to travel to the site of St. Claire's Defeat (Battle of the Wabash) on December 12, 1793. He planned to launch an assault against the Wabash tribes in the spring and wanted to use the site as an area to stage his troops and supplies.

December 25, 1793 - Wayne's Forces Reach Site of St. Claire's Defeat

The detachment sent by General Wayne reached the site of St. Claire's Defeat on December 25, 1793. The soldiers found the skeletons of the hundreds of men that died in the battle scattered about the site of the battlefield. They pitched their tents at the site. On December 26, the soldiers buried the remains of the fallen soldiers and proceeded to build a fort, which General Wayne would call Fort Recovery.

January 1794

January 15, 1794 - Indiana Governor Noah Noble Born

Noah Noble (January 15, 1794 – February 8, 1844)

Elizabeth Clair Sedgwick Noble presented her husband, Dr. Thomas Noble, with their new son on January 15, 1794 in Berryville, Virginia. Noah was one of fourteen children born to the couple. The family migrated to Campbell County, Kentucky in 1800, where Dr. Noble opened a medical practice. At seventeen, Noah joined his brother, James, in Brookville, Indiana. His brother had a successful law practice in Brookville and later became a Senator to the United States Senate from Indiana.

Businessman

From 1811 Noah operated several businesses around Brookville. These included a hotel; water powered weaving mill and a trading company. The trading company purchased produce from farmers in the Brookville area. They exported this produce to New Orleans for sale there. A boating accident in 1819 ended this business, in which he lost an entire shipment. The debt incurred by this disaster left him indebted for many years. He married Catherine Stull that same year. The couple had three children, two of which died young.

Military

Following his business venture, he enlisted in the 7th Regiment of the Indiana militia unit in 1819. He became a lieutenant colonel, eventually gaining promotion to colonel in 1820.

Politics

His first foray into politics was a run for sheriff of Franklin County in 1820. He won this election handily and after his term ended, he won an easy election to the Indiana House of

Representatives in 1824. He gained a position with the Indiana Land Office in Indianapolis from 1825 to 1829. In this position he collected money from land sales in the state for the Federal Government. He helped on the Michigan Road project, a major road connecting Lake Michigan with the Ohio River. In 1830 he gained the nomination for governor of Indiana as a Whig.

Whig Party

The Whigs were a major political party early in the Nineteenth Century. They espoused rapid economic and industrial growth. Their philosophy advocated government support for a free market system, and encouraged business people with skill and expertise. They wanted a superior bank credit system, high tariffs, a business-oriented money supply based on a national bank. Strong supporters of internal improvements, they advocated a strong infrastructure of roads and canals. They also favored a system of public schools, private colleges, charities, and cultural institutions. They were opposed by the Democratic Party, which advocated an egalitarian agricultural society. They believed that modernization led to the development of a powerful aristocratic class which would threaten democracy. During this period, Whigs tended to be more successful on the State level, while Democrats on the national level.

Governor (Dec 07, 1831 - Dec 06, 1837)

As a Whig, Noble was a strong proponent of internal improvements in the state. His most notable achievement was passage of the Mammoth Internal Improvement Act in 1836. He recommended a tax increase to pay for the act, a recommendation the Legislature failed to enact. This failure proved unfortunate for the State of Indiana and fatal for the Whig Party in Indiana. The massive debt incurred by the expenses of the bill forced the State into bankruptcy after the

Panic of 1837 and led to the demise of the Whig party in Indiana.

Retirement

The failure of the Mammoth Internal Improvement Act in 1836 was a political disaster for Noble, who retired to private life at the end of his term. He died in Indianapolis in 1844 and is interred in Crown Hill Cemetery. Noble County, in northeast Indiana, is named in his honor.

February 19, 1794 - James Brown Ray - Indiana Governor (1794-1848)

The fourth governor of Indiana, Ray accomplished a number of "firsts" during his tenure in office and be the last non-partisan governor.

James Brown Ray (February 19, 1794 – August 4, 1848)

The son of Revolutionary War Veteran Reverend William Ray and Phebe Ann Brown Ray, James was native to Jefferson County, Kentucky. After attending local public schools, Ray migrated to Cincinnati, Ohio to study law. After passing the bar, he served as clerk of the Hamilton County courts briefly before marrying Mary Riddle and moving to Brookville, Indiana. He and Mary had two children before Mary died in 1823. He established a law office in Brookville and married Esther Booker, with whom he would have five children.

Politics

Ray's belligerent personality made him popular among the people, who elected him to the Indiana House of Representatives, followed by election to the Indiana Senate in 1822. When Lieutenant Governor Ratliff Boon resigned to become a United States Representative, the Senate elected Ray as Senate Pro Tempore on the same day.

Governor

Lieutenant Governor William Hendricks became governor after Boon's resignation. Hendricks resigned as governor in 1825 after his election to the United States Senate. Senate Pro Tempore Ray became governor, as the Lieutenant Governor position had been left open, the only person ever elevated to the governorship from the Senate Pro Tempore position. At 31 years old, he was also the youngest man to serve in that post. He would gain election as governor by the voters to a three year term in 1825. During his term, the state capitol moved to Indianapolis, making him the first governor to serve in the new capital city. The first couple refused to live in the governor's mansion, charging that it lacked privacy. Ray won his reelection bid in 1828, making him the longest serving governor of Indiana during the tenure of the 1816 Constitution.

Later Life

Ray's belligerent personality led him into many conflicts during his term of office. He ended his second term having accomplished little. He had failed in a bid to have the legislature elect him as a United States Senator. His early advocacy of railroads over canals led to derision. Detractors also derided his vision of the new capital city serving as a hub of railroad transportation. During his term he also concluded treaties with the Pottawattamie and Miami Indian tribes. After leaving office, he attempted to practice law in Indianapolis with little success. Moves to Greencastle and Centerville had similar results. His already eccentric behavior became worse. He carried a cane and would periodically stop and write in the air with it. During a trip to Wisconsin he fell ill with cholera. He went to Cincinnati to stay with relatives, where he died on August 4, 1848.

March 1794

Early March 1794 - Fort Recovery Complete

General Wayne's force at the site of St. Clair's Defeat finished construction of the fort built on the battle site in early March 1794. The fort, constructed to withstand the strongest attack by Amerindian warriors, received a garrison of 250 soldiers commanded by Major Henry Burbeck.

April 1794

April 1794 - British Begin Constructing Fort Miamis

The British defied the 1783 Treaty of Paris with the Americans by commencing construction of a fort in American territory at the rapids of the Maumee River.

Reasons:

The British wanted to continue their lucrative fur trade with the Amerindians

They wanted to forestall American dominance in the region

British Governor Simcoe feared that General Wayne would move against Detroit, which the British had refused to abandon, also in defiance of the Treaty

The new fort, Fort Miamis, would provide an obstacle to American advance

The fort would encourage the Amerindian tribes in their war with the United States

Sometime in April British troops arrived at the site, in the current city of Maumee, Ohio, and began construction of the fort. Located about ten miles from the point where the Maumee River empties into Lake Erie in extreme northwestern Ohio, the fort would was a formidable British presence in American territory.

Amerindians Encouraged

The construction of the British fort encouraged the various tribes that were engaged in conflict with the United States. They hoped that war would break out between the two nations, a war which would certainly help their cause. During the months preceding the fort's construction various initiatives had taken place to hold more peace conferences. However, when the British began construction on the fort, the native tribes abandoned the effort. Hoping for British military aid in their war, they continued gathering warriors and planning for war.

April 1794 - Land Office Virginia Military District Opens

Virginia had ceded the vast stretch of land that became the Northwest Territory to Congress in 1784 to encourage passage of the Articles of Confederation. In exchange, Congress had allowed Virginia to a large section of land between the Little Miami and Scioto Rivers in current south-central Ohio. This land Virginia could use to grant land to grant to Virginia's Revolutionary War veterans as payment for their service. Surveyors began surveying this large tract in the 1780's, however the first land grants did not take place until 1794. The Military District granted land in the region until 1803, when Ohio became a state. The Hamilton County Recorder's Office opened in April 1794 to record land sale transactions, mortgage records, births, deaths and other information.

June 1794

June 29, 1794 - Convoy Departs Fort Greenville for Fort Recovery

On the morning of June 29, 1794 a supply convoy led by Major William McMahan departed from Fort Greenville. By evening the convoy had covered the thirty miles of trail to Fort Recovery. The convoy included 360 packhorses loaded with supplies, which was defended by fifty dragoons and ninety riflemen. By nightfall the convoy arrived at Fort Recovery. The fort lacked space for the entire force to stay inside, so many of the soldiers camped outside the fort. During the evening a friendly Indian warrior entered Fort Recovery and warned the commander of the fort that a large number of warriors had gathered in the forests outside the fort. The commander laughed off the warning.

June 29, 1794 - British and Indian Force Arrive at Fort Recovery

Large numbers of Indian warriors began gathering in the region of Au Glaize during the days of early summer, 1794. Indian chiefs Blue Jacket and Little Turtle were the leaders of this disparate force of warriors. By late June they totaled around 2500 warriors from many different tribes. Since the warriors needed to hunt to obtain sustenance, the large force was hard to manage as they had to break up into smaller groups. Squabbles between many of the tribes broke out, putting stress on the loose alliance. With great difficulty, Little Turtle and Blue Jacket began moving the large force towards Fort Recovery with hopes of uncovering the cannon St. Clair's forces had hidden after the Battle of the Wabash in November 1792. A force of British soldiers and officers accompanied the natives, bringing a quantity of gunpowder and shot to use in the recovered cannons against the force occupying Fort Recovery. This force moved into position on the evening of June 29, as the convoy of supplies arrived at Fort Recovery, the site of their earlier success.

June 30, 1794 - Little Turtle Attacks Fort Recovery Supply Train

The supply convoy departed Fort Recovery during in the morning, taking the trail back to Fort Greenville. When the 150 man convoy reached a point about 1000 feet from the fort the largest force of Amerindian warriors ever gathered in North America attacked. Little Turtle, Blue Jacket and Simon Girty led the attack which numbered around 2500 warriors. Tecumseh, a young Shawnee chief that would play a prominent role in later struggles, also participated in the attack.

The Battle

A large contingent of the 2500 warriors had concealed themselves in the forest along both sides of the trail. When the convoy had penetrated well into the waiting warriors trap, they attacked. They wounded or killed fifteen of the soldiers and managed to capture 300 packhorses. The commander of Fort Recovery heard the sounds of battle and sent a contingent of troops out to rescue the troops. The dragoons accompanying the convoy managed to cut a route through the attacking Indians, allowing the remaining soldiers to retreat to the protection of the fort.

After the Attack

Inside the fort the defenders, numbering about 250 soldiers, waited for an attack they feared would come. Outside, the leaders of the Amerindian force met. Many believed they should attack the fort while others did not. At length, they decided that since the attack on the convoy had been successful, they would mount an assault on the fort the next day.

July 01, 1794 - Battle of Fort Recovery

During the evening hours American scouts reported that there were many British soldiers embedded in the large force that now laid siege to Fort Recovery. The Amerindian force attacked while it was still dark, however the 250 soldiers inside the fort held fast. Several hours later the warriors retreated from the walls. About four hours later, they attacked again. Once more, the soldiers resisted the attack, leading the Amerindian force to depart. Fort Recovery had held. Twenty three soldiers died in the assault and another twenty-nine wounded. The natives captured three soldiers. Amerindian loss estimates range from seventeen to fifty.

July 26 - 1794 - General Scott Joins Wayne's Forces

Major General Charles Scott arrived at Greenville with 1500 mounted militia troops. The arrival of Scott's force from Kentucky brought Wayne's total troop strength up to 3500 soldiers. General Wayne was ready to move.

July 28, 1794 - General Wayne Begins March from Greenville

General Wayne along with 2000 of his troops and 900 of the Kentucky Volunteers commanded by General Scott departed Fort Greenville at 8:00 AM on July 28, 1794. The Legion marched in front of the column with the volunteers falling in behind. The first night the army marched twelve miles and camped on the banks of Stillwater Creek. The soldiers felled trees to make a breastwork about 600 yards square for protection against attack. The beginning of the march had been through bushy country; however it became marshy as they neared the creek. The soldiers marched ankle deep in mud.

July 29, 1794 - Wayne's Army Reaches Fort Recovery

At about 3:00 PM the army reached Fort Recovery. Fifteen cannon stationed in the North and the East blockhouses fired a salute at the army's approach. They continued on past the fort to a spot about a mile from the fort on the northwest bank of the Wabash River and camped, taking the same defensive measures as they had the night before. Wayne ordered the halt in order to allow the baggage wagons to catch up with the main body of troops. The swift pace of the march had fatigued the dragoons, whose horses had received some injuries as they moved through the thick forests at the edge of the road where the dragoons marched as they protected the flank of the army.

July 31, 1794 – Wayne's Troops Halt to Build Bridge over Beaver Creek

Wayne's army marched about eleven miles on July 30, reaching Beaver Creek on July 30. The army halted to build a bridge across the creek at a camp they would name Camp Beaver Swamp. The weather had been hot and dry, thus the troops could find no running water. The bridge needed to be seventy feet long and would be five feet wide. Construction of the bridge proved to be an exhausting task for the troops, however by 8:00 AM the next morning. On the same day a group of 100 men went out in advance, guarded by a strong contingent of troops, to cut a road for the army to use to the St. Mary's River, which was twelve miles away. Soldiers complained of a plaque of mosquitoes that caused much discomfort.

August 1794

August 01, 1794 - Wayne's Troops Reach St. Mary's River

Wayne's troops crossed the bridge they had built with few problems and preceded along the road the contingent, called the Pioneers in the journals the author is using as a source, quickly. All of these journals mention the fertility of the soil and the beauty of the prairie through which they pass. They pass small groves of trees one of the writer's felt had been left to divide fields, of which evidence is in plenty. The army marched about eleven miles, reaching the St. Mary's River, at which the General calls a halt. General Wayne decided the site would be a good place to build a garrison, so had the army set up camp on the south side of the river. After sending out scouts to reconnoiter, he decided to build it on the north side, so the troops gathered their things and crossed the river, which was about fifty feet wide at this point. They camped in two lines, both parallel to the river, with guards on the flank to protect the main body of troops and the supplies. The water was not good to drink, however many of the soldiers took the opportunity to bathe in its waters. They would remain in camp for about three days, building the garrison.

August 02, 3, 1794 - Army In Camp

The army remained in camp for two days erecting the fort General Wayne would christen Fort Adams, in honor of the current Vice President of the United States. While in camp some of the soldiers sewed blankets together and commenced using them as nets to catch fish from the river. The catch included perch, pike, salmon, trout as well as a variety of other fresh water fish. The troops dined on fresh fish as they worked building the fort. The hot, dry weather continued unabated as they continued their task. On August 2 General Wayne dispatched William Wells and Captain

Ephraim Kibbey out on a spying mission with a small number of soldiers. Wells suggested that if Wayne gave him 200 soldiers he would attempt to take some prisoners; however the General demurred, instead opting for the smaller force. One incident of note occurred on August 3 when a large beech tree fell on the commander's wagon, nearly killing him. However, the General was only slightly hurt in the accident. The diarists note that on August 2 a small band of natives appeared and apparently captured one soldier and one horse. William Wells, in company with Captain Ephraim Kibbey, returned from a spy mission on the 3rd and reported seeing the band retreating with what they presumed the captive in custody. A supply convoy arrived on August 3, commanded by a Brigadier General Barbee bringing a large quantity of supplies for the encamped army.

August 07, 1794 - Wayne's Troops Reach Au Glaize River

General Wayne ordered the march to begin again at six o'clock in the morning. He left about 100 men, forty of them invalids, to garrison Fort Adams, which was not complete. The blockhouses had not been chinked nor had roofs put on. The commander of the garrison, Lieutenant James Underhill, feared that the unfinished stockade invited attack. The trees that he and his men would need to complete the construction were a considerable distance from the fort. Wayne's troops marched through thickly forested land with excellent soil. They marched ten miles on August 4, twelve miles on the 5 and about twelve miles on August 6 though this type of country. They camped each night by late afternoon. The only drinking water they could find in the boggy areas was to dig a hole in the soil, wait for the mud to clear and dip the water out of the hole. On August 8, 1794 the army reached Delaware Creek, which they crossed. Here they occupied one of the towns on the Au Glaize River. The natives had abandoned the town in the face of Wayne's advance. Wayne's spies reported in to note that they were within ten or twelve miles of the site that served as the Northern Indian Confederacy's headquarters. The spies reported that the natives had abandoned these towns also, leaving their vegetable plots and corn fields open to the predations of Wayne's troops. The army camped along the picturesque river, which was about one hundred yards wide at this point. They had covered ten miles and were about sixty-eight miles from Fort Recovery.

August 08, 1794 - Wayne's Troops Occupy Amerindian Headquarters

The troops marched eight miles from their camp on the Auglaize River to the junction of that river with the Maumee. The beauty of the country along with the quantity and variety of maize and vegetables astounded them. Soldiers on the scene estimated that over 1000 acres of maize surrounded the villages along with vegetables of every description. On the way, they marched through the first rain that fell during their journey. The native settlements in the region consisted of small clusters of villages perched on high ground overlooking the river. Extensive vegetable gardens surrounded these villages.

The Legion camped on the west bank of the Au Glaize at the point the rivers meet. General Scott's Kentucky Volunteers camp opposite the Legion on the north side of the Maumee while the Flankers camped on the east side of the Auglaize. Wayne's spies report that the natives are camped about two miles from the British garrison, Fort Miami, which was about fifty miles from Wayne's camp on the Maumee.

At 5:00 Wayne had the guns discharged in honor of their advance. The troops then set about building extensive earthworks.

August 09, 1794 - General Wayne's Troops Begin Building Fort

General Anthony Wayne decided that his troops would build a garrison at the junction of the two rivers, the former headquarters of the Northwest Indian Confederacy. He drew up a plan for the fortress and deployed troops to cut timbers and clear the site. The fort's location provided an excellent view upriver and downriver of the Maumee. The general also ordered that the horses and cattle be turned loose in the extensive corn fields. Thus, he began the process of destroying the natives' food supply. The soldiers, upon searching the villages surrounding the site, found evidence that the former inhabitants of the village had departed in a great hurry. They found brass cooking pots and other cooking implements scattered about in the weeds. Woodworking tools like hammers, augers and chisels suggested that whites also inhabited the village. Great quantities of vegetables of many types were found in the gardens adjacent to many of the small log cabins that served as homes. Wayne also dispatched foraging parties to scour the surrounding countryside for food to sustain the hungry army.

August 10, 1794 - General Wayne Dispatches Spies

Work began on the fort that General Wayne would call Fort Defiance, with soldiers cutting the pickets which were to be at least fifteen feet long and twelve inches in diameter on the smallest end. The troops were in good spirits and well fed with meat and vegetables. General Wayne dispatched

Captain William Wells, Henry Miller and Captain Robert McClellan and few others to approach the enemy to gather intelligence and take some prisoners, if possible.

Robert McClellan (1770-November 22, 1815)

The son of James and Martha McCoy McClelland, Robert was native to Mercersburg, Pennsylvania. His education was limited; however Robert became well schooled hunting and frontier survival. He worked as a pack horseman before joining the army as a scout in 1790. His first post was at Fort Gower, which was located at the confluence of the Hocking and Ohio Rivers downstream from Hockingport, Ohio. In 1791 he was sent to Fort Washington at Cincinnati. At Fort Washington he assisted with running the pack horse trains that ran between Fort Hamilton and Fort Washington. When General Anthony Wayne arrived with the Legion of the United States to engage in his campaign against the Northwest Amerindian tribes, he employed McClellan as a spy and scout.

August 12, 1794 - William Wells and Robert McClellan Return with Prisoners

William Wells, Henry Miller and Captain Robert McClellan had approached within a short distance of the almost completed British Fort Miamis at the rapids of the Maumee River. They noted smoke rising from a campfire on a piece of high ground near the Au Glaize River. The campsite was located in the middle of a clearing that prevented the three men from approaching too close, however they perceived three warriors camped by the fire. The men noted a log located within a rifle shot from the camped warriors and crept stealthily towards it.

The Plan

Once there, they devised a plan. Wells and Miller would choose a target and kill him. McClellan would, at the sound of the shots, run down the remaining warrior and capture him.

Capture

The plan went as planned, with the remaining warrior running from the camp, close pursued by McClellan. When the warrior approached the river, he jumped from a high bluff into it. McClellan jumped after him. The warrior's feet sank in the muck, allowing McClellan to approach him. McClellan had a tomahawk with which he threatened the warrior, who first drew his knife, decided to surrender.

Surprise

While washing the mud from his body, Henry Miller perceived that the prisoner was his brother, Christopher. The brothers had been taken prisoner years before. Henry had escaped and joined the service of General Wayne as a scout. McClellan was wounded in the shoulder during the brief struggle. They captured two women and three men, one of which was a white man taken prisoner and adopted into the tribe. During interrogation Miller revealed that the soldier taken on August 2 had not been taken prisoner, rather he had defected. He had relayed to the natives a great deal of information about Wayne's force, including their strength and order of march. They also related that the natives were committing a great deal of energy to assembling the forces of various tribes. The Pottawattamie had not yet joined with the force in great numbers, however. The prisoners related that forty warriors died during the battle at Fort Recovery on July 1.

August 13, 1794 - Wayne's Troops Complete Fort Defiance

The troops completed the construction of the fort that Wayne called Fort Defiance on August 13. The general had determined to make one last effort at making peace, so he dispatched Christopher Miller, the man taken prisoner the day before, to carry a message to the native camp. The message stated that General Wayne had ten native prisoners, several men and two women, held safely at Fort Greenville and that if they harmed Miller, they would hang the prisoners. The message also contained one last appeal for peace. Miller departed from the fort, bound for the Amerindian camp carrying the message.

Christopher Bryan Miller (1768-1828)

The son of Ernest and Margaret Lindeman Miller, the family had migrated to Hardin County, Kentucky while Christopher and his brother Henry were children. The boys were captured by a band of Shawnee warriors in 1783. During their captivity, Christopher learned the Shawnee language as well as three other native tongues. In 1792 Henry escaped. Before he ran away, he tried in vain to convince Christopher to go with him. Christopher remained with the Shawnee until captured by his brother Henry on August 12, 1794.

Mid August, 1794 - British Complete Fort Miamis

Sometime in early to mid August 1794 the British completed construction on Fort Miamis. The fort consisted of four diamond shaped bastions with a twenty-five foot trench completely surrounding the fort. The British lined the trench with sharpened stakes to resist any attack by an enemy force. Fourteen strategically placed cannon completed the defenses of the fort. The British garrisoned about 450 troops in the fort, which would remain in place for almost eighteen years.

August 13, 1794 - Wayne Sends Miller Out with Letter Asking For Peace

On August 13, General Anthony Wayne decided to make one last overture for peace. He drafted a letter that stated that the natives had been deluded by the "Bad and designing men," at the base of the falls to wage war. The war had led Wayne and his army to occupy their villages and settlements. He invited the tribes to appoint men to meet him at Roche Le Bout, which was a rock in the middle of the Maumee River the natives used as a council site, to discuss terms of peace. He warned the natives to not harm his messenger or he would hang the native prisoners he had in his possession at Fort Greenville. He gave this letter, and a white flag of peace, to Christopher Miller to carry to the native chiefs.

August 15, 1794 - Legion of the United States Resumes March

General Anthony Wayne ordered the troops to resume their march into Amerindian country on August 15, 1794. The army proceeded about nine miles, camping at a considerably large native village called Snaketown, which is the current site of Florida, Ohio on the banks of the Maumee River. They marched along many large fields of corn, vegetables and other crops planted by the natives in soil that appeared quite fertile.

August 16, 1794 - Wayne Received Reply to His Appeal for Peace

The army resumed marching at dawn and moved about nine miles, when General Wayne ordered a halt at about three o'clock in the afternoon to camp along the river bank. The weather had continued extremely hot and dry. Christopher Miller returned to report the Indian's reply to General Wayne. Their encampments was near the new British Fort Miamis, which Miller believed was providing supplies to the Indians in camp, which Miller estimated to be about a thousand warriors. A Chief White Eyes, the commander of the encampment, returned the General's good wishes and noted that the warriors had just been making preparations to meet them when Miller brought his message. The chief offered to come and meet with the general to discuss peace if he would remain the Au Glaize for ten days and not build any new forts. Wayne declined to answer the reply and ordered the march to resume the following morning.

August 18, 1794 - Wayne's Forces Reach Rocke De Bout

August 17 the army had passed through marched about twelve miles without incident. An express company overtook the army during the march carrying letters and reports from Washington. The army rose at dawn on August 18 and began its march at 6:00 AM. Though expecting attack as they approached the enemy's camp at Rocke De Bout at any instant, they proceeded unhindered and arrived at that spot in mid afternoon. During the march they passed numerous cabins, pleasant gardens and fields. They discovered account books and silversmith tools, evidence of British from Detroit living among the natives. William Clark describes Rocke De Bout as a small island in the middle of the Maumee River that was of considerable height. A small grove of cedar trees occupied the tip of the island. The rapids at this point provided a ford which the army could cross. Clark reports that a there was lovely view of the surrounding prairie from the summit of the island. After their arrival, Wayne sent out five men to spy out the countryside; however they encountered a large force of warriors. The presence of the natives compelled the spies to retreat, however the Indians did capture one of the men. As the army bunked down for the night, every man expected that on the morrow the native force would attack.

August 19, 1794 - Wayne Builds Fort Deposit

Constantly under the threat of an attack, General Wayne decided to build a temporary fort in which to deposit the army's heavy equipment to make the troops more mobile. Thus, troops spent most of the day constructing this fortification and stowing the equipment and supplies inside. Upon completion of the fort, which the general called Fort Deposit, Wayne issued orders that the army would march at 6:00 AM the following morning. Morale among the troops was high and the soldiers were confident that, if attacked, they would defeat the enemy.

August 19, 1794 Indian Chiefs Hold Council - Prisoner Executed

The natives had captured one of Wayne's spies on August 18, a man whose last name was May. They discovered that the man had once lived among them and spoke their language. They threatened that because he did not choose to continue living among them that they would kill him the next morning. They followed through of the promise by tying him to a large oak tree and making a mark on his breast. The man died as scores of bullets riddled his body.

Council

The Amerindian force had made camp in a place along the Maumee River in which the trees had been felled by some terrible force of nature, possibly a tornado. The chiefs of the tribes held a council to decide what to do about Wayne's forces. Wayne's army had occupied their main town, destroyed their crops and threatened to continue the policy. Wayne's continued success also threatened their alliance with the British, whose support for their cause cooled somewhat after the Confederacy's defeat at Fort Recovery. After that battle, some of the natives had second thoughts about attacking the force led by General Wayne. Many of the chiefs, Blue Jacket among them, favored attacking them. Little Turtle, however spoke in opposition to attacking Wayne.

Little Turtle Abandons the Confederacy

Little Turtle, the most respected and experienced of the Amerindian chiefs, spoke of caution and urged that they consider General Wayne's offer of peace. Calling Wayne the "general that never sleeps," he noted it would be difficult to launch a surprise attack on this force as they had some of previous generals they had defeated. Wayne kept his army on the move and always had spies about to gather intelligence. He warned that although they had scored stunning victories over two previous generals, they could not expect to always have the same result. As he concluded his remarks, many of the chiefs joined him. However, many others agreed with Blue Jacket. Little Turtle had concluded that it would be suicide for his tribe of Shawnee to attack the Americans and abandoned the confederacy. Many others followed him. Thus, Blue Jacket, the leader of this confederate force, had only about four or five hundred warriors left, a much depleted force than that that had attacked Fort Recovery in June. The combined Legion of the

United States and General Scott's experienced frontier fighters totaled about three thousand.

August 20, 1794 - Battle of Fallen Timbers

A thunderstorm prevented the army from commencing its march until seven o'clock. They reached the site of the Amerindian's planned ambush in the fallen timbers area around eight o'clock. The river flows from southwest to northeast at this point. The Maumee River lay to the right, the fallen timbers area to the left as the advance guard entered a flood plain between the river and the fallen trees.

Fire Fight

A fierce fire erupted as the warriors opened a fusillade of lead at the troops. The advance guard, hit hard by concentrated fire from a superior number of adversaries, retreated to the main body of troops. When the first shots rang out, Wayne ordered General Scott's mounted volunteers to circumvent the enemy's right wing and come at them from the rear. Additionally, he ordered the cavalry to advance into the open prairie between the attackers and the river.

Bayonet Charge

Lastly, he ordered a bayonet charge by the front line of troops against the center line of enemy positions. Riflemen supported the action by firing at enemy positions using buck and ball shot, which tended to wound the targets rather than kill. This type of shot caused the natives more problems than actual deaths. During the course of this battle, Lieutenant William Henry Harrison rode furiously back and forth while under fire relaying orders from General Wayne to his subordinates and carrying their messages to him. The only officers killed during the action were a Captain Campbell and a Lieutenant Towles.

No Refuge

The chiefs had hoped that the fallen trees would provide adequate cover for the warriors; however the ferocity of the attack drove the natives from the field before the cavalry completed their task of surrounding them. They fled back towards the British Fort Miamis, with Wayne's forces in hot pursuit. Upon reaching this supposed site of sanctuary, the British commander instead refused them entry, fearing provoking a war with the United States at a time that Britain had a war going on with France.

Disappearing Attackers

With a superior enemy pursuing them close behind and the British fort closed to them, the confederacy's disappointed and incensed warriors simply disbanded and disappeared into the forest, never to trust British promises again. A young warrior named Tecumseh, who fought during this battle, would in later years challenge Wayne's Aide-de-Camp, William Henry Harrison, the future Indiana Territorial Governor and General William Henry Harrison. Harrison used the lessons learned from General Wayne and Wilkinson during this campaign and used them later in his career. General Wayne's forces closed in on the fort and encamped in sight of the walls. Wayne had his soldiers taunt the British by parading them in front of the walls. The British refused to take the bait and attack.

About forty Amerindian warriors fell in the battle and an equal number of Americans, with about eighty wounded.

August 21, 1794 - Wayne's Remain Encamped at Fort Miamis

General Wayne's army remained encamped just about a half mile from the walls of the British Fort Miamis. Many of the troops feared that they would receive orders to attack the fort, which would have been a difficult assignment given the impressive nature of the fortification. By late afternoon the commander of the fort, Major William Campbell, sent a message to General Anthony Wayne under a flag of truce. In the letter he noted that he was surprised to see an American army camped so near "his Majesty's cannons."

Wayne's Answer

Wayne sent an answer that expressed surprise that news of the affair between Wayne's army and the native force the day before so near the fort hadn't gotten to him and that had he allowed the warriors to take refuge in the fort, its walls and cannon would have offered the British no protection.

Encamped

The army remained encamped near the fort's walls, destroying the fields of corn, the gardens and burning copious quantities of hay stored near the fort's walls. The troops also burned the cabins that occupied the area around the fort.

All the while General Wayne pondered the possibility of storming the fort.

August 22, 1794 - Wayne's Forces Pillage Area Around Fort Miamis

Wayne's forces continued to burn the cabins, crops and property of the Canadians and Amerindians that had established a village outside the fort. Wayne had four companies of light troops and four companies of dragoons accompany him to within 100 yards of the fort. Wayne inspected the fort from every angle and concluded that he would need heavy artillery, which he did not have, to capture the fort, so he decided against assaulting it. The commander of the fort sent a delegation carrying a flag of truce to confer with the general and demanded that he withdraw from the fort. Wayne demanded that the commander surrender the fort, as it was on United States territory. The commander refused. Thus, at a stalemate, Wayne's troops continued their destruction. Wayne's spies scoured the countryside, searching for the Amerindian force that had attacked them.

August 23, 1794 - Wayne's Troops Celebrate Their Victory, Honor the Dead

Wayne's spies could find no evidence of the natives anywhere in the immediate area. Evidently they had abandoned their villages all along the Maumee, even the ones near its mouth at the lake. General Wayne gave a short speech congratulating the troops for their achievement of defeating an enemy that had the support of Canadian militia and a British fort immediately at their rear. At noon Wayne caused fully charged cannon to be fired three times in honor of those that had fallen in the battle. The sounding of the cannon signaled that it was time for the troops to return the way they came and take up camp at Fort Deposit.

August 27, 1794 - Wayne's Troops Return to Fort Defiance

The army continued marching back the way they had come, destroying any of the native's crops and cabins as they could find on the route. They reached the Miami River and the site of Fort Defiance at about noon on August 27. Troops in the fort fired their cannon in recognition of their arrival. The troops marched about a half mile from the fort, threw up the usual fortifications and made camp, about half of the force on each side of the river. The soldiers wounded during the battle, having survived the three day journey in litters and on horseback, had been sent forward to the fort on the 26th.

September 1794

September 13, 1794 - Captain Ephraim Kibbey Sent Out to Construct a Road Towards Kekionga

Captain Ephraim Kibbey and his company started forward early in the morning to guard a company of road builders to clear a trace towards Kekionga. At 8:00 AM the main army departed. General Wayne left a garrison of about 300 men to occupy the fort. Additionally he gave a letter to a captured Amerindian woman who was to help guide the road builders. The letter contained another appeal for peace. Four men deserted the army and disappeared into the forest.

September 13, 1794 - Symmes Purchase

John Cleves Symmes had petitioned the government for one million acres of land in 1788; however he did not receive title for these lands until September 13, 1794, when President George Washington signed the deed. Further, Congress did not approve the sale of one million acres, instead allowing him to purchase 311,682 acres. The patent reserved from the sale the fifteen acre Fort Washington site and one square mile of land near the mouth of the Great Miami River. It also reserved sections in each township for schools, religion and land for Congress future needs. Unfortunately for Congress, and Symmes, he had sold off some land not included in the final transaction before he owned it. Much of this land was outside his patent, thus many people had purchased land from Symmes that he did not gain title to. He also used an unusual land survey method that did not adhere to standards set by Congress. Congress later addressed the latter problem by allowing the settlers who had purchased land from Symmes first chance at buying their lands from the Federal Government, thus gaining legal title. The Symmes Purchase made it clear to Congress that it must utilize government surveyors to establish base lines and corners before selling land. It also conducted no more large scale land purchases like Symmes.

September 17, 1794 - Legion of the United States Arrived at Kekionga

After marching for three days through marshy, wet countryside along the Maumee River, the army reached Kekionga, at the junction of the St. Mary's and St. John's Rivers. General Wayne decided to build a fort at this strategic junction, a key connection point between the Great Lakes to the north and the portage to the Wabash River to the south.

The Portage

During the late Seventeenth and early Eighteenth Century the Miami tribe controlled one of the most valuable pieces of real estate in the Ohio River Valley. The area between the St. Mary's River and Wabash River proved the shortest portage point between two great waterways, the Great Lakes and the Mississippi River. The portage, or "carrying place" in French, allowed travelers moving by water access to the Mississippi River from the St. Lawrence River and beyond. The French utilized the portage, at the pleasure of the Miami, during their early explorations into the North American interior. The Miami realized the importance of the portage, as it had been used by Amerindian tribes for centuries. The tribe allowed their friends, the French, to use it, after paying a toll.

The Importance of the Portage

Traveling by canoe, a traveler could voyage from Lake Erie up the Maumee River to the junction of three rivers, the Maumee, St. Joseph and St. Mary's. From the junction, the route turned southeast on the St. Mary's to the portage point. Canoeists needed only carry their canoes a short distance, which varied by the season of the year, only a few miles from the portage point on the St. Mary's River to the Wabash. Once in the Wabash a traveler could journey down the Wabash to the Ohio and on to the Mississippi. The French used to portage point to move goods from their colonies in New France to New Orleans. The Amerindians used it to move the furs they collected to their trading partners further east. All these travelers had to pass through the lands of the Miami Indians, who collected a toll from everyone.

Arrival

The last fourteen miles had been a forced march. About four pack horses a day died from the immense effort and lack of forage. Many of the wagons broke down as well. The army crossed the Maumee and encamped on the northwest side of the Maumee at the junction.

September 17, 1794 - Four British Deserters Arrive at Wayne's Camp

Wayne's troops busied themselves erecting fortifications. Supplies had not been getting through, so they were on half rations. The commander of Fort Defiance sent four deserters from the British Fort Miamis to Wayne. According to the deserters, a sizable group of natives were still encamped near the fort, however many of these left every day. They also noted that the Amerindians kept about twenty warriors following Wayne's force and were now talking about making peace. They also said that the British fort had a garrison of about 250 men, that many were sick and that the fort had a good supply of munitions.

September 19, 1794 - Ground Cleared for Construction of a Fort

The troops, who had been on half rations and no ration of salt, had been working on clearing ground for the construction of a fort just below the junction of the St. Mary's and St. Joseph Rivers, the source of the Maumee. The site was favorable, as it allowed a commanding view of all three rivers.

September 22, 1794 - Wayne Begins Construction of Fort Wayne

The troops suffered through a lack of provisions, remaining on half rations and deprived of salt. Preparations for the construction of the fort continued and on September 21, a shipment of about 40,000 rations of flour arrived. On the same day the General Wayne reviewed the troops. Afterwards they attended a church service officiated by Pastor Dr. Jones. A company of dragoons that General Wayne had sent out in pursuit of some deserters returned to the camp, not having discovered the deserters or the enemy. Heavy rains had fallen on the 19th and 20th, raising the level of the rivers.

On the morning of September 22 a detachment of about 250 men began construction of the fort. They hitched logs to the backs wagons and drug them to the construction site, fashioning the logs with axes and adzes and commenced building. The lack of forage and heavy work led to the deaths of about four horses a day.

Four men deserted from the camp sometime during the day, absconding with the horses of three officers.

September 26, 1794 - Searchers Find Two Deserters Killed

Searchers dispatched to find the soldiers that had deserted their posts in the days since they had begun construction of the fort. They found two of them near Snaketown, killed and scalped. They also discovered signs that Amerindian warriors had camped about three miles from their camp. The searchers had gone as far as Fort Defiance. The searchers brought back letters from the commander of that post informing Wayne that eighteen men had deserted that post. Wayne sent Ephraim Kilby out with a company of men to gather intelligence about their location.

September 28, 1794 - Warriors Attack Party on Trail

A small supply convoy arrived at the camp on September 28 with a herd of 120 cattle. The officer in charge of the convoy reported that a party of soldiers and some women came under attack by Amerindian warriors somewhere in between Fort Recovery and Fort Greenville. The party, in company with a General Todd, had been traveling to Fort Greenville to acquire supplies. Three soldiers died in the attack. One soldier and a woman were taken prisoner. William Clark notes in his journal that one horse died in the attack, a horse that had been a particular favorite of his, a Chickasaw horse he had sent back to Fort Greenville. Later in the day Clark, in company with General James Willkinson rode out to the site of the October 19, 1790 Hardin's Defeat. They found the country "open and pleasantly situated."

September 30, 1794 - Supplies Arrive at Camp

General Todd arrived with a small shipment of supplies, letters and other papers.

October 1794

October 02, 1794 - Rebellion in the Camp

General Wayne ordered General Thomas Barbee to take his Volunteer Brigade and March to Fort Greenville to fetch provisions. The men, tired of the work and privation of life on the frontier, refused to march and demanded to be taken home, instead. General Wayne, upon hearing of the near mutiny, visited the brigade and told them that if they did not obey orders, he would report them to the War Office as "revolters," and they would forfeit their pay. His warning calmed the rebellious men down. Wayne issued an extra gill, about five ounces, of whiskey to each of them as payment. The brigade departed the next morning for Fort Greenville, however the soldiers in the brigade continued in a semi-mutinous state, stealing from the other soldiers and creating problems.

October 14, 1794 - General Scott's Volunteers Depart

The construction of the fort had proceeded along well. General Barbee's volunteers had departed on October 3 and Captain Butler had left on October 9 with forty dragoons. The troops had completed construction of a small sloop named the *Ataway*, which had departed camp on the Maumee on October 10. The sloop struck a rock about a mile from the camp and capsized. The boat was righted; however it lost the greater part of its cargo of flour. General Scott's troops buried two men that had died after which they departed the camp for Fort Defiance on October 24.

October 24, 1794 - Lieutenant Colonel Hamtramck Takes Command

By October 24, 1794 the troops had constructed the barracks, which formed the fort's walls, and blockhouse, which overlooked the river. General Wayne appointed Lieutenant Colonel Hamtramck as the commandant of the fort. Hamtramck opened the fort with a ceremony at 8:00 AM that included the firing of fifteen cannons as he dubbed the new garrison Fort Wayne, after which six companies of men chosen by him marched into the fort to take up their stations. The fort's location gave it a commanding view of the native villages beyond. The difficulty of moving adequate supplies for the troops over the long, difficult trail leading from Fort Washington had led to shortages of many items, including shoes and other sundry supplies. The native warriors had continued to harass isolated companies near Fort Defiance. An attack on October 20 had led to the deaths of seven whites and thirty Indians. Fort Defiance suffered a number of desertions. One man, caught, was tried and hung on October 14. General Wayne had the soldiers begin making preparations for the march back to Fort Greenville.

October 26, 1794 - General Wayne's Troops Depart Fort Wayne

General Wayne's troops began the long journey through the prairie and forest at 11:00 AM on October 26. The Legion would travel southeast along the St. Mary's River through Northeastern Indiana, entering the future state of Ohio in east central Adams County, Indiana. They would continue southeast for several days until they met the trace they had cut earlier on their route north from Fort Greenville.

November 02, 1794 - Wayne's Troops Return to Fort Greenville

General Wayne' troops arrived back at Fort Greenville on November 2, 1794. The troops marched in accompanied by a salute of fifteen cannon and fifteen platoon guns. After parading about the fort, the army broke formation and occupied their former quarters that they had held the previous July when they began the campaign. The campaign, begun on July 28, had concluded. After the troops had returned, General Wayne dispatched peace emissaries to invite the tribal leaders to a conference to discuss terms of peace.

December - 1794 - Tribal Leaders Meet at Fort Wayne to Begin Peace Efforts

The inability of the native force, the largest Amerindian force ever assembled, to defeat the Americans at the Battle of Fort Recovery on July 1 and the defeat at Fallen Timbers on August 20 had demoralized the greater part of the natives. Wayne had located a strong fort, Fort Wayne, within sight of their principal village, Kekionga, and had burned a large part of their food stores. He had also had his troops destroy many of their villages. Thus, deprived of their food and with no shelter, the Amerindians faced a long, cold, hungry winter.

More Settlers Arrive

The natives also noted that the number of settlers that were entering their territory north of the Ohio River were too numerous for them to resist. Historical lore indicates that sometime after Wayne's return to Fort Greenville, an influential Miami leader visited General Wayne offering a gift meant to convey his intentions to pursue peace. Since Little Turtle had begun advocating for peace after the native's defeat at the Battle of Fort Recovery, many historians believe that this chief was Little Turtle. In early December two native leaders visited Fort Wayne and reassured the commander of that post that the Amerindians were ready to pursue peace. Thus, the New Year opened with the prospect of the end of the Northwest Indian War.

Acknowledgements

January 01, 1792 - Early Indiana

https://scholarworks.iu.edu/journals/index.php/imh/article/view/6327/6370

The Battle Of The Wabash And The Battle Of Fort Recovery:

Christine K. Thompson, Principal Investigator

Erin A. Steinwachs

Kevin C. Nolan, Co-Principal Investigator

https://www.bsu.edu/-
/media/www/departmentalcontent/aal/aalpdfs/abpp%20composite%20map%20docum
ent%20final.pdf?la=en

January 30, 1792 - Lieutenant Colonel James Wilkinson Relief Mission Arrives Fort
Jefferson

William Henry Harrison and the Conquest of the Ohio Country: Frontier ...

By David Curtis Skaggs

https://books.google.com/books?id=nWzeAgAAQBAJ&pg=PA26&lpg=PA26&dq=wilkin
son+fort+jefferson+january+1792&source=bl&ots=sWBehp96Pb&sig=7BBJ8kNNlUIIKprE
PiKTu0eI7mY&hl=en&sa=X&ved=2ahUKEwiNnb-h6qveAhXK34MKHUP7B-
QQ6AEwAnoECAcQAQ#v=onepage&q=wilkinson%20fort%20jefferson%20january%2017
92&f=false

http://wardepartmentpapers.org/document.php?id=6210

https://en.wikipedia.org/wiki/St._Clair%27s_Defeat

By Charles Theodore Greve

https://books.google.com/books?id=eJxABLtxX60C&pg=PA250&lpg=PA250&dq=wilkins
on+arrives+battle+site+january+1792&source=bl&ots=e8b7_KqUC4&sig=ShDv1oOXqmhB
dQyUojjs5FsHVts&hl=en&sa=X&ved=2ahUKEwju5dfjptHeAhXL4IMKHdJAAKUQ6AEw
B3oECAkQAQ#v=onepage&q=wilkinson%20arrives%20battle%20site%20january%201792
&f=false

January 24, 1792 - Wilkinson Departs for Fort Jefferson

William Henry Harrison and the Conquest of the Ohio Country: Frontier ...

By David Curtis Skaggs

https://books.google.com/books?id=nWzeAgAAQBAJ&pg=PA26&lpg=PA26&dq=wilkin
son+fort+jefferson+january+1792&source=bl&ots=sWBehp96Pb&sig=7BBJ8kNNlUIIKprE
PiKTu0eI7mY&hl=en&sa=X&ved=2ahUKEwiNnb-h6qveAhXK34MKHUP7B-
QQ6AEwAnoECAcQAQ#v=onepage&q=wilkinson%20fort%20jefferson%20january%2017
92&f=false

Centennial History of Cincinnati and Representative Citizens, Volume 1

By Charles Theodore Greve

https://books.google.com/books?id=eJxABLtxX60C&pg=PA250&lpg=PA250&dq=wilkins
on+arrives+battle+site+january+1792&source=bl&ots=e8b7_KqUC4&sig=ShDv1oOXqmhB
dQyUojjs5FsHVts&hl=en&sa=X&ved=2ahUKEwju5dfjptHeAhXL4IMKHdJAAKUQ6AEw
B3oECAkQAQ#v=onepage&q=wilkinson%20arrives%20battle%20site%20january%201792
&f=false

February 01, 1792 - Wilkinson Arrives at the Battle Site

William Henry Harrison and the Conquest of the Ohio Country: Frontier ...

By David Curtis Skaggs

https://books.google.com/books?id=nWzeAgAAQBAJ&pg=PA26&lpg=PA26&dq=wilkin
son+fort+jefferson+january+1792&source=bl&ots=sWBehp96Pb&sig=7BBJ8kNNlUIIKprE
PiKTu0eI7mY&hl=en&sa=X&ved=2ahUKEwiNnb-h6qveAhXK34MKHUP7B-
QQ6AEwAnoECAcQAQ#v=onepage&q=wilkinson%20fort%20jefferson%20january%2017
92&f=false

Centennial History of Cincinnati and Representative Citizens, Volume 1

By Charles Theodore Greve

https://books.google.com/books?id=eJxABLtxX60C&pg=PA250&lpg=PA250&dq=wilkins
on+arrives+battle+site+january+1792&source=bl&ots=e8b7_KqUC4&sig=ShDv1oOXqmhB
dQyUojjs5FsHVts&hl=en&sa=X&ved=2ahUKEwju5dfjptHeAhXL4IMKHdJAAKUQ6AEw
B3oECAkQAQ#v=onepage&q=wilkinson%20arrives%20battle%20site%20january%201792
&f=false

February 11, 1792 - Indians Attack Hunting Party at Fort Jefferson

The Soldiers of America's First Army, 1791

By Richard M. Lytle

https://books.google.com/books?id=UDxBU0JfgjMC&pg=PA212&lpg=PA212&dq=comm
ander+fort.+St.+Clair+1792&source=bl&ots=4pmgInuBW6&sig=hmR9N4MQbMiYINeDaY
9im2T2Ltc&hl=en&sa=X&ved=2ahUKEwiO0ey0ifLfAhWE2YMKHbxcC2cQ6AEwCHoEC
AEQAQ#v=onepage&q=commander%20fort.%20St.%20Clair%201792&f=false

March 05, 1794 - Congress Aproves Act Creating the Legion of the United States

Historical Register and Dictionary of the United States Army: From ..., Volume 1

By Francis Bernard Heitman

https://books.google.com/books?id=DqLcgTjCR_wC&pg=PA139&lpg=PA139&dq=legio
n+of+the+united+states+formed+1792&source=bl&ots=Ozp5DtXWwl&sig=_tW2ROwX3-
rJ5tVuFVa9cUgHT0k&hl=en&sa=X&ved=2ahUKEwjFoez769jeAhUG3YMKHf0NB08Q6AE
wCXoECAMQAQ#v=onepage&q=legion%20of%20the%20united%20states%20formed%20
1792&f=false

https://en.wikipedia.org/wiki/Dragoon

https://armyhistory.org/the-battle-of-fallen-timbers-20-august-1794/

https://en.wikipedia.org/wiki/Legionville

March 1793 - Fort St. Clair Constructed

http://uncledeanshistory.weebly.com/fort-jefferson-ohio.html

https://www.hmdb.org/marker.asp?marker=19152

March 14, 1792 - John Francis Hamtramck Negotiates Treaty with Natives

http://wardepartmentpapers.org/document.php?id=6355

A History of Indiana, from Its Earliest Exploration by Europeans to the ...

By John Brown Dillon

https://books.google.com/books?id=aTAUAAAAYAAJ&pg=PA290&lpg=PA290&dq=ale
xander+trueman+mission+1792&source=bl&ots=eK8BXy8F_P&sig=LoZJkL5YTLrgwYyDI
bSOGI8xaA0&hl=en&sa=X&ved=2ahUKEwi3wOSureXeAhUB44MKHdM0CYQQ6AEwB3
oECAIQAQ#v=onepage&q=alexander%20trueman%20mission%201792&f=false

March 30, 1792 - St. Claire Requests Court Martial

http://wardepartmentpapers.org/document.php?id=6424

April 07, 1792 - St. Claire Resigns Commission

http://www.ohiohistorycentral.org/w/St._Clair%27s_Defeat

April 07, 1792 - Wilkinson Dispatches Two Peace Missions

By Indiana Historical Society

https://books.google.com/books?id=aTAUAAAAYAAJ&pg=PA290&lpg=PA290&dq=ale
xander+trueman+mission+1792&source=bl&ots=eK8BXy8F_P&sig=LoZJkL5YTLrgwYyDI
bSOGI8xaA0&hl=en&sa=X&ved=2ahUKEwi3wOSureXeAhUB44MKHdM0CYQQ6AEwB3
oECAIQAQ#v=onepage&q=alexander%20trueman%20mission%201792&f=false

https://en.wikipedia.org/wiki/Columbia-Tusculum,_Cincinnati

By David Andrew Nichols

https://books.google.com/books?id=xl5dDwAAQBAJ&pg=PT176&lpg=PT176&dq=Alexa
nder+Trueman++destination+"1792"&source=bl&ots=yKyVZdyLMv&sig=OrXGAdGNFqI
SzuBPbj93a_8GknE&hl=en&sa=X&ved=2ahUKEwiM9LzFiPzeAhULP6wKHUX9BrAQ6AE
wDXoECAQQAQ#v=onepage&q=Alexander%20Trueman%20%20destination%20"1792"&f
=false

April 15, 1792 - Trueman and Freeman Parties Separate

American State Papers: Documents, Legislative and Executive, of ..., Volume 9

https://books.google.com/books?id=c7UbAQAAMAAJ&pg=PA312&lpg=PA312&dq=maj
or+trueman+destination+1792&source=bl&ots=4kkNG_bglR&sig=WesaLQp_h_UCnJqiEgt
QGvFR2sQ&hl=en&sa=X&ved=2ahUKEwjz1rvmhPzeAhUIbq0KHUmpB1YQ6AEwD3oEC
AIQAQ#v=onepage&q=major%20trueman%20destination%201792&f=false

April 16 - 1792 - Isaac Freeman, John Gerard, and John Hardin Killed

https://founders.archives.gov/documents/Washington/05-14-02-0021

https://www.jstor.org/stable/27790263?read-
now=1&loggedin=true&seq=4#page_scan_tab_contents

http://wardepartmentpapers.org/document.php?id=7145

Joseph Gerard (1763 - 1792)

https://www.geni.com/people/Joseph-Garard/6000000070269663050

http://www.uh.edu/~jbutler/gean/josephgerrard.html

April 17, 1792 - William Smalley Before King Boconjehaulis

https://books.google.com/books?id=V1JIAAAAYAAJ&pg=PA298&lpg=PA298&dq=alexa
nder+trueman+mission+1792&source=bl&ots=tWqWPBO0Jt&sig=-
ZnRcK_Duo7dEJVG20HxBGuyCfY&hl=en&sa=X&ved=2ahUKEwjuqcOnt-
XeAhUL7YMKHZ9TCLY4ChDoATAAegQIARAB#v=onepage&q=alexander%20trueman
%20mission%201792&f=false

William Smalley (c.1762 - September 30 1838)

https://www.findagrave.com/memorial/29265883/william-crawford

https://www.wikitree.com/wiki/Smalley-9

http://home.earthlink.net/~wrj2/data/pg9.html

Rufus Putnam (April 9, 1738 – May 4, 1824)

The Memoirs Of Rufus Putnam

https://books.google.com/books/about/The_Memoirs_of_Rufus_Putnam_and_Certain.ht
ml?id=uZY0AAAAIAAJ

April 18, 1792 - Joseph Gerard's Head Brought into Camp

Indiana Historical Society Publications, Volume 1

By Indiana Historical Society

https://books.google.com/books?id=V1JIAAAAYAAJ&pg=PA298&lpg=PA298&dq=alexa
nder+trueman+mission+1792&source=bl&ots=tWqWPBO0Jt&sig=-
ZnRcK_Duo7dEJVG20HxBGuyCfY&hl=en&sa=X&ved=2ahUKEwjuqcOnt-
XeAhUL7YMKHZ9TCLY4ChDoATAAegQIARAB#v=onepage&q=alexander%20trueman
%20mission%201792&f=false

https://www.geni.com/people/Joseph-Garard/6000000070269663050

Early May - 1792 - Smalley Reunited With His Indian Father

Indiana Historical Society Publications, Volume 1

By Indiana Historical Society

https://books.google.com/books?id=V1JIAAAAYAAJ&pg=PA298&lpg=PA298&dq=alexa
nder+trueman+mission+1792&source=bl&ots=tWqWPBO0Jt&sig=-
ZnRcK_Duo7dEJVG20HxBGuyCfY&hl=en&sa=X&ved=2ahUKEwjuqcOnt-
XeAhUL7YMKHZ9TCLY4ChDoATAAegQIARAB#v=onepage&q=alexander%20trueman
%20mission%201792&f=false

https://www.geni.com/people/Joseph-Garard/6000000070269663050

May 05, 1792 - Rufus Putnam Appointed Brigadier General

THE MEMOIRS OF RUFUS PUTNAM

https://books.google.com/books/about/The_Memoirs_of_Rufus_Putnam_and_Certain.ht
ml?id=uZY0AAAAIAAJ

Rufus Putnam (April 9, 1738 – May 4, 1824)

The Memoirs Of Rufus Putnam

https://books.google.com/books/about/The_Memoirs_of_Rufus_Putnam_and_Certain.ht
ml?id=uZY0AAAAIAAJ

May 10, 1792 - Hendrick Aupaumut Departs Philadelphia

Captain Aupaumut A Short Narration of My Last Journey to the Western Country,
Page 40

https://archive.org/stream/memoirshistoric06penngoog#page/n71/mode/2up/search/a
upaumut

May 18, 1792 - John Heckeweller Receives Letter Requesting Aid in Crafting Treaty

John Heckewelder's Journey to the Wabash

https://ia801702.us.archive.org/12/items/jstor-20083232/20083232.pdf

John Heckeweller (March 12, 1743 - January 31, 1823)

https://www.ohiohistory.org/visit/museum-and-site-locator/schoenbrunn-village

http://colonialquills.blogspot.com/2015/12/christmas-at-schoenbrunn-in-1773.html

http://www.ohiohistorycentral.org/w/David_Zeisberger

https://en.wikipedia.org/wiki/David_Zeisberger

https://en.wikipedia.org/wiki/John_Heckewelder

John Heckewelder's Journey to the Wabash i

https://ia801702.us.archive.org/12/items/jstor-20083232/20083232.pdf

http://www.ohiohistorycentral.org/w/John_G._Heckewelder

http://explorepahistory.com/hmarker.php?markerId=1-A-22B

http://snaccooperative.org/ark:/99166/w69k4fjj

The Travels of John Heckewelder in Frontier America

By Paul A. Wallace

https://books.google.com/books?id=HjLoIo0wdesC&pg=PA34&lpg=PA34&dq=John+He
ckewelder+1754+father&source=bl&ots=pDAFhpklz4&sig=XRq7Ut4cCr8_16PLKvCBrwsJi
g0&hl=en&sa=X&ved=2ahUKEwi285XH3pffAhVqooMKHVgUAbQ4FBDoATADegQICB
AB#v=onepage&q=John%20Heckewelder%201754%20father&f=false

https://www.geni.com/people/John-Heckewelder/6000000038044816378

https://allthingsliberty.com/2018/06/a-curious-trial-on-the-frontier-zeisberger-
heckewelder-et-al-vs-great-britain/

https://www.ohiohistory.org/visit/museum-and-site-locator/schoenbrunn-village

http://colonialquills.blogspot.com/2015/12/christmas-at-schoenbrunn-in-1773.html

http://www.ohiosfirstvillage.com/

The Life of John Heckeweller

David Zeisberger (April 11, 1721 – November 17, 1808)

https://www.ohiohistory.org/visit/museum-and-site-locator/schoenbrunn-village

http://colonialquills.blogspot.com/2015/12/christmas-at-schoenbrunn-in-1773.html

http://www.ohiohistorycentral.org/w/David_Zeisberger

https://en.wikipedia.org/wiki/David_Zeisberger

https://www.ohiohistory.org/visit/museum-and-site-locator/schoenbrunn-village

http://colonialquills.blogspot.com/2015/12/christmas-at-schoenbrunn-in-1773.html

http://www.ohiosfirstvillage.com/

Hendrick Aupaumut (1757-1830)

https://www.findagrave.com/memorial/75678217/hendrick-aupaumut

https://en.wikipedia.org/wiki/Hendrick_Aupaumut

https://collections.dartmouth.edu/occom/html/ctx/personography/pers0257.ocp.html

http://wardepartmentpapers.org/document.php?id=6664

https://allthingsliberty.com/2016/02/the-stockbridge-mohican-community-1775-1783/

https://en.wikipedia.org/wiki/Mahican

https://allthingsliberty.com/2016/02/the-stockbridge-mohican-community-1775-1783/

American State Papers: Documents, Legislative and Executive, of the Congress ...

By United States. Congress

May 25, 1792 - Hendrick Aupaumut Meets with Joseph Brandt

https://www.newyorkroots.org/ontario/1893hist%20Canantown.htm

Historical Index to the Pickering Papers

By Massachusetts Historical Society

https://books.google.com/books?id=2K5yAAAAMAAJ&pg=PA82&lpg=PA82&dq=Hend
rick+Aupaumut+Canandaigua+1792+may&source=bl&ots=EgHRCllAVH&sig=ACfU3U2l
GHnyXE-MPEJ98R-
A2KaPwvoHLQ&hl=en&sa=X&ved=2ahUKEwjV6dOlpobgAhWB5YMKHYQlAN4Q6AE
wDXoECAgQAQ#v=onepage&q=Hendrick%20Aupaumut%20Canandaigua%201792%20
may&f=false

May 26, 1792 - Heckeweller Departs Bethlehem

John Heckewelder's Journey to the Wabash

https://ia801702.us.archive.org/12/items/jstor-20083232/20083232.pdf

June 02, 1792 - William Henry Harrison Promoted to Lieutenant

William Henry Harrison and the Conquest of the Ohio Country: Frontier ...

By David Curtis Skaggs

https://books.google.com/books?id=nWzeAgAAQBAJ&pg=PA26&lpg=PA26&dq=wilkin
son+fort+jefferson+january+1792&source=bl&ots=sWBehp96Pb&sig=7BBJ8kNNIUIIKprE
PiKTu0eI7mY&hl=en&sa=X&ved=2ahUKEwiNnb-h6qveAhXK34MKHUP7B-
QQ6AEwAnoECAcQAQ#v=onepage&q=wilkinson%20fort%20jefferson%20january%2017
92&f=false

Van Buren, Harrison, Tyler, Polk, Taylor, Fillmore, Pierce, Buchanan, Lincoln

By John Fiske

https://books.google.com/books?id=qdQvAQAAMAAJ&pg=PA33&lpg=PA33&dq=1793
+harrison+aide-de-
camp+wayne+june&source=bl&ots=iYgi6U09g_&sig=V0rCd8Yu0A7rZ4WsdCLIyzKasLs&
hl=en&sa=X&ved=2ahUKEwj4-

fb676bfAhWG4IMKHbqoCDkQ6AEwBXoECAQQAQ#v=onepage&q=1793%20harrison%2
0aide-de-camp%20wayne%20june&f=false

June 08, 1792 - Heckeweller Arrives Pittsburg

John Heckewelder's Journey to the Wabash

https://ia801702.us.archive.org/12/items/jstor-20083232/20083232.pdf

June 08, 1792 - Heckeweller and Putnam Depart on Peace Mission

John Heckewelder's Journey to the Wabash

https://ia801702.us.archive.org/12/items/jstor-20083232/20083232.pdf

https://en.wikipedia.org/wiki/Washington,_Pennsylvania

June 11, 1792 - Heckeweller and Putnam Reach Marietta

John Heckewelder's Journey to the Wabash

https://ia801702.us.archive.org/12/items/jstor-20083232/20083232.pdf

https://en.wikipedia.org/wiki/Campus_Martius_(Ohio)

https://en.wikipedia.org/wiki/Picketed_Point_Stockade

Benjamin Tupper (March 11, 1738 - June 16, 1792)

https://en.wikipedia.org/wiki/Benjamin_Tupper

http://www.ohiohistorycentral.org/w/Benjamin_Tupper

https://www.geni.com/people/Brevet-Brig-General-Benjamin-Tupper-Continental-Army/6000000012535061681

https://www.encyclopedia.com/history/encyclopedias-almanacs-transcripts-and-maps/tupper-benjamin

https://www.history.com/this-day-in-history/battle-of-brewster-island

https://www.bostonmagazine.com/news/2014/07/31/throwback-thursday-battles-boston-light/

Nathanial Massie (December 28, 1763 - November 03, 1813)

http://www.ohiohistorycentral.org/w/Nathaniel_Massie

https://www.geni.com/people/Nathaniel-Massie/6000000041318565023

Joseph Shaylor (October 23, 1746 - March 04, 1816)

https://www.geni.com/people/Lieutenant-Joseph-Shaylor/6000000024337018974

https://www.wikitree.com/wiki/Shaylor-39

https://www.findagrave.com/memorial/105231431/joseph-shaylor

The Soldiers of America's First Army, 1791

By Richard M. Lytle

https://books.google.com/books?id=UDxBU0JfgjMC&pg=PA212&lpg=PA212&dq=comm
ander+fort.+St.+Clair+1792&source=bl&ots=4pmgInuBW6&sig=hmR9N4MQbMiYINeDaY
9im2T2Ltc&hl=en&sa=X&ved=2ahUKEwiO0ey0ifLfAhWE2YMKHbxcC2cQ6AEwCHoEC
AEQAQ#v=onepage&q=commander%20fort.%20St.%20Clair%201792&f=false

https://journals.psu.edu/pmhb/article/viewFile/40939/40660

The Soldiers of America's First Army, 1791

By Richard M. Lytle

https://books.google.com/books?id=UDxBU0JfgjMC&pg=PA212&lpg=PA212&dq=comm
ander+fort.+St.+Clair+1792&source=bl&ots=4pmgInuBW6&sig=hmR9N4MQbMiYINeDaY
9im2T2Ltc&hl=en&sa=X&ved=2ahUKEwiO0ey0ifLfAhWE2YMKHbxcC2cQ6AEwCHoEC
AEQAQ#v=onepage&q&f=false

Quartermaster support of the Army: a history of the corps, 1775-1939

By Erna Risch

https://books.google.com/books?id=7FH3wb1DqNIC&pg=PA108&lpg=PA108&dq=shayl
or+october+1793+supplies+attacked&source=bl&ots=qsMYMCx8nR&sig=ACfU3U2jwooE
b9gVhfM2oMrnX_yFaLZeHA&hl=en&sa=X&ved=2ahUKEwiM7beEq53iAhXSmq0KHRz2
DEAQ6AEwAnoECAgQAQ#v=onepage&q=shaylor%20october%201793%20supplies%20a
ttacked&f=false

June 25, 1792 – Hay Cutter's Massacre

http://uncledeanshistory.weebly.com/fort-jefferson-ohio.html

Fallen Timbers 1794: The US Army's first victory

By John F. Winkler

https://books.google.com/books?id=hFmbCwAAQBAJ&pg=PA10&lpg=PA10&dq=fort+j
efferson+1792+june+25+attack&source=bl&ots=Bwb_L8epSo&sig=ACfU3U0R0lYH5dizP5
hcWVnDFNUCAc7mIg&hl=en&sa=X&ved=2ahUKEwj_-
5_1mfffAhXk1IMKHZcJBJAQ6AEwC3oECAIQAQ#v=onepage&q=fort%20jefferson%2017
92%20june%2025%20attack&f=false

June 26, 1792 - Heckeweller and Putnam Depart Marietta

John Heckewelder's Journey to the Wabash

https://ia801702.us.archive.org/12/items/jstor-20083232/20083232.pdf

https://www.cityofbelpre.com/history/

https://en.wikipedia.org/wiki/Farmer%27s_Castle

June 27, 1792 - Heckeweller and Putnam Arrive Gallipolis

http://www.wvencyclopedia.org/articles/725

John Heckewelder's Journey to the Wabash i

https://ia801702.us.archive.org/12/items/jstor-20083232/20083232.pdf

https://en.wikipedia.org/wiki/Burning_Springs,_West_Virginia

http://www.wvexp.com/index.php/Burning_Springs,_West_Virginia

June 28, 1792 - Heckeweller and Putnam in Gallipolis

https://ia801702.us.archive.org/12/items/jstor-20083232/20083232.pdf

John Heckewelder's Journey to the Wabash i

https://en.wikipedia.org/wiki/Gallipolis,_Ohio

June 30, Peace Expedition Reach Cincinnati

John Heckewelder's Journey to the Wabash i

https://ia801702.us.archive.org/12/items/jstor-20083232/20083232.pdf

https://www.northamericanforts.com/East/oh-sw.html#hamilton

https://en.wikipedia.org/wiki/Manchester,_Ohio

John Heckewelder's Journey to the Wabash

https://ia801702.us.archive.org/12/items/jstor-20083232/20083232.pdf

July 04, 1792 - Joseph Shaylor Reinstated by By General Wayne

https://books.google.com/books?id=UDxBU0JfgjMC&pg=PA212&lpg=PA212&dq=comm
ander+fort.+St.+Clair+1792&source=bl&ots=4pmgInuBW6&sig=hmR9N4MQbMiYINeDaY
9im2T2Ltc&hl=en&sa=X&ved=2ahUKEwiO0ey0ifLfAhWE2YMKHbxcC2cQ6AEwCHoEC
AEQAQ#v=onepage&q=commander%20fort.%20St.%20Clair%201792&f=false

William Wells (c. 1770 – August 15, 1812)

https://www.jstor.org/stable/27790311?seq=1#page_scan_tab_contents

Wednesday, April 3, 2019

https://scholarworks.iu.edu/journals/index.php/imh/article/download/10110/13932/0

William Wells: Frontier Scout and Indian Agent Paul A. Hutton"

https://scholarworks.iu.edu/journals/index.php/imh/article/view/10110/13932

John Heckewelder's Journey to the Wabash i

Indiana's Timeless Tales - 1792 – 1794

https://ia801702.us.archive.org/12/items/jstor-20083232/20083232.pdf

July 16, 1792 - Chief Jean Krouch Died

American State Papers: Documents, Legislative and Executive, of the Congress ...

By United States. Congress

https://books.google.com/books?id=hbWsTT4Mdr0C&pg=PA239&lpg=PA239&dq=chief
+died+fort+washington+july+16+1792&source=bl&ots=WZ2oOScp6T&sig=K20vJw5rcwr1
R6iAKkdQznmI1ho&hl=en&sa=X&ved=2ahUKEwjs2Kam3e_fAhWHxYMKHZmlDsAQ6
AEwDHoECAMQAQ#v=onepage&q=chief%20died%20fort%20washington%20july%2016
%201792&f=false

https://ia801702.us.archive.org/12/items/jstor-20083232/20083232.pdf

John Heckewelder's Journey to the Wabash

July 17, 1792 - Chief Jean Krouch Funeral

John Heckewelder's Journey to the Wabash i

https://ia801702.us.archive.org/12/items/jstor-20083232/20083232.pdf
        https://books.google.com/books?id=hbWsTT4Mdr0C&pg=PA239&lpg=PA239
&dq=chief+died+fort+washington+july+16+1792&source=bl&ots=WZ2oOScp6T&sig=K20
vJw5rcwr1R6iAKkdQznmI1ho&hl=en&sa=X&ved=2ahUKEwjs2Kam3e_fAhWHxYMKHZ
mlDsAQ6AEwDHoECAMQAQ#v=onepage&q=chief%20died%20fort%20washington%20j
uly%2016%201792&f=false

July 19, 1792 - Indian Prisoners Confer with Putnam

John Heckewelder's Journey to the Wabash i

https://ia801702.us.archive.org/12/items/jstor-20083232/20083232.pdf

Francis Vigo (1747 - March 22, 1836)

John Heckewelder's Journey to the Wabash

https://archive.org/details/jstor-20083258/page/n1

https://en.wikipedia.org/wiki/Six_Mile_Island_State_Nature_Preserve

http://www.louisvilleareacanoeandkayak.org/paddling_the_ohio.php

July 22, 1792 - Letter from Rufus Putnam to Secretary Knox

American State Papers: Documents, Legislative and Executive, of the Congress ...

By United States. Congress

https://books.google.com/books?id=hbWsTT4Mdr0C&pg=PA239&lpg=PA239&dq=chief
+died+fort+washington+july+16+1792&source=bl&ots=WZ2oOScp6T&sig=K20vJw5rcwr1
R6iAKkdQznmI1ho&hl=en&sa=X&ved=2ahUKEwjs2Kam3e_fAhWHxYMKHZmlDsAQ6

AEwDHoECAMQAQ#v=onepage&q=chief%20died%20fort%20washington%20july%2016
%201792&f=false

July 22, 1792 - Soldier Punished for Rebellion
John Heckewelder's Journey to the Wabash i
https://ia801702.us.archive.org/12/items/jstor-20083232/20083232.pdf

August 06, 1792 - Indians Attack
John Heckewelder's Journey to the Wabash i
https://ia801702.us.archive.org/12/items/jstor-20083232/20083232.pdf

August 10, 1792 - Escorts for Indian Prisoners Arrive Fort Washington
John Heckewelder's Journey to the Wabash i
https://ia801702.us.archive.org/12/items/jstor-20083232/20083232.pdf

August 11, 1792 - Military Supplies Arrive at Fort Washington
John Heckewelder's Journey to the Wabash i
https://ia801702.us.archive.org/12/items/jstor-20083232/20083232.pdf

August 13, 1792 - Indian Attack
John Heckewelder's Journey to the Wabash i
https://ia801702.us.archive.org/12/items/jstor-20083232/20083232.pdf

August 18, 1792 - Putnam and Heckewelder Depart for Vincennes

https://www.jstor.org/stable/27790263?read-
now=1&loggedin=true&seq=8#page_scan_tab_contents

August 20, 1792   Heckeweller and Putnam Reach Fort Steuben
John Heckewelder's Journey to the Wabash i
https://ia801702.us.archive.org/12/items/jstor-20083232/20083232.pdf
https://en.wikipedia.org/wiki/Six_Mile_Island_State_Nature_Preserve
http://www.louisvilleareacanoeandkayak.org/paddling_the_ohio.php

August 21, 1792 - The Putnam Party Traverses the Falls of the Ohio

John Heckewelder's Journey to the Wabash

https://archive.org/details/jstor-20083258/page/n1

August 22, 1792 - Heckeweller's Description of the Falls

John Heckewelder's Journey to the Wabash

https://archive.org/details/jstor-20083258/page/n1

September 2, 1792 - The Putnam Party Reaches The Wabash River

John Heckewelder's Journey to the Wabash

https://archive.org/details/jstor-20083258/page/n1

September 04, 1792 - Anthony Wayne Announces the Formation of the Legion of the United States

Historical Register and Dictionary of the United States Army: From ..., Volume 1

By Francis Bernard Heitman

https://books.google.com/books?id=DqLcgTjCR_wC&pg=PA139&lpg=PA139&dq=legio n+of+the+united+states+formed+1792&source=bl&ots=Ozp5DtXWwl&sig=_tW2ROwX3-rJ5tVuFVa9cUgHT0k&hl=en&sa=X&ved=2ahUKEwjFoez769jeAhUG3YMKHf0NB08Q6AE wCXoECAMQAQ#v=onepage&q=legion%20of%20the%20united%20states%20formed%20 1792&f=false   https://armyhistory.org/the-battle-of-fallen-timbers-20-august-1794/

September 12, 1792 - Putnam and Heckewelder Arrive Vincennes

The Potawatomis: Keepers of the Fire

By R. David Edmunds

https://books.google.com/books?id=aKgKCioMi9wC&pg=PA125&lpg=PA125&dq=tribes +vincennes+september+1792&source=bl&ots=A99fQOad0Z&sig=ACfU3U1e3TJnGe5bwyl BM4ubpZXtJJo5FA&hl=en&sa=X&ved=2ahUKEwiokoD0sujgAhUD2oMKHQa5CXU4ChD oATABegQIARAB#v=onepage&q=tribes%20vincennes%20september%201792&f=false

https://www.jstor.org/stable/27790263?read-now=1&loggedin=true&seq=8#page_scan_tab_contents

https://founders.archives.gov/documents/Washington/05-11-02-0192

September 13, 1792 - Putnam Releases Indian Prisoners to their Tribes

https://www.jstor.org/stable/27790263?read-now=1&loggedin=true&seq=8#page_scan_tab_contents

John Heckewelder's Journey to the Wabash

https://archive.org/details/jstor-20083258/page/n1

September 19, 1792 - Drovers Arrive With Cattle - Food for Treaty Attendees

https://www.jstor.org/stable/27790263?read-now=1&loggedin=true&seq=8#page_scan_tab_contents

https://www.jstor.org/stable/27790263?read-now=1&loggedin=true&seq=8#page_scan_tab_contents

John Heckewelder's Journey to the Wabash

September 24, 1792 - Negotiations Begin Treaty of Vincennes

https://www.jstor.org/stable/27790263?read-now=1&loggedin=true&seq=8#page_scan_tab_contents

September 27, 1792 - Treaty of Vincennes Signed

https://www.jstor.org/stable/27790263?read-now=1&loggedin=true&seq=8#page_scan_tab_contents

A History of Indiana, from Its Earliest Exploration by Europeans to the ...

By John Brown Dillon

https://books.google.com/books?id=aTAUAAAAYAAJ&pg=PA290&lpg=PA290&dq=ale
xander+trueman+mission+1792&source=bl&ots=eK8BXy8F_P&sig=LoZJkL5YTLrgwYyDI
bSOGI8xaA0&hl=en&sa=X&ved=2ahUKEwi3wOSureXeAhUB44MKHdM0CYQQ6AEwB3
oECAIQAQ#v=onepage&q=alexander%20trueman%20mission%201792&f=false

https://founders.archives.gov/documents/Washington/05-11-02-0192

The Potawatomis: Keepers of the Fire

By R. David Edmunds

https://books.google.com/books?id=aKgKCioMi9wC&pg=PA125&lpg=PA125&dq=tribes
+vincennes+september+1792&source=bl&ots=A99fQOad0Z&sig=ACfU3U1e3TJnGe5bwyl
BM4ubpZXtJJo5FA&hl=en&sa=X&ved=2ahUKEwiokoD0sujgAhUD2oMKHQa5CXU4ChD
oATABegQIARAB#v=onepage&q=tribes%20vincennes%20september%201792&f=false

September 28, 1792 - Putnam Becomes Sick With Fever

John Heckewelder's Journey to the Wabash

https://archive.org/details/jstor-20083258/page/n1

September 29, 1792 - Indians Stage Celebration

John Heckewelder's Journey to the Wabash

https://archive.org/details/jstor-20083258/page/n1

September 30, 1792 - Grand Council at the mouth of the Auglaize River

The Battle Of The Wabash And The Battle Of Fort Recovery:

Christine K. Thompson, Principal Investigator

Erin A. Steinwachs

Kevin C. Nolan, Co-Principal Investigator

https://www.bsu.edu/-
/media/www/departmentalcontent/aal/aalpdfs/abpp%20composite%20map%20docum
ent%20final.pdf?la=en

https://en.wikipedia.org/wiki/Fort_St._Clair

https://founders.archives.gov/documents/Washington/05-11-02-0164

Alexander McKee (1738 - January 05, 1799)

https://en.wikipedia.org/wiki/Alexander_McKee

https://www.geni.com/people/Col-Alexander-McKee/6000000003265684425

September 30, 1792 - Gifts Distributed to the Indians

https://philadelphiaencyclopedia.org/archive/treaty-negotiations-with-native-
americans/

John Heckewelder's Journey to the Wabash

https://archive.org/details/jstor-20083258/page/n1

Early 1792 - William Smalley's Hunting Trip

Indiana Historical Society Publications, Volume 1

By Indiana Historical Society

https://books.google.com/books?id=V1JIAAAAYAAJ&pg=PA298&lpg=PA298&dq=alexa
nder+trueman+mission+1792&source=bl&ots=tWqWPBO0Jt&sig=-
ZnRcK_Duo7dEJVG20HxBGuyCfY&hl=en&sa=X&ved=2ahUKEwjuqcOnt-
XeAhUL7YMKHZ9TCLY4ChDoATAAegQIARAB#v=onepage&q=alexander%20trueman
%20mission%201792&f=false

Early October, 1792 - Smalley's Brother's Injury Foils their Plan

https://books.google.com/books?id=V1JIAAAAYAAJ&pg=PA298&lpg=PA298&dq=alexa
nder+trueman+mission+1792&source=bl&ots=tWqWPBO0Jt&sig=-
ZnRcK_Duo7dEJVG20HxBGuyCfY&hl=en&sa=X&ved=2ahUKEwjuqcOnt-
XeAhUL7YMKHZ9TCLY4ChDoATAAegQIARAB#v=onepage&q=alexander%20trueman
%20mission%201792&f=false

October 05, 1792, Heckeweller Begins Journey Along Buffalo Trace

John Heckewelder's Journey to the Wabash

https://archive.org/details/jstor-20083258/page/n1

October 09, 1792 - Heckeweller Party Reaches Buffalo Salt (French) Lick

John Heckewelder's Journey to the Wabash

https://archive.org/details/jstor-20083258/page/n1

October 11, 1792 - Heckeweller Party Overtaken by Thunderstorm

John Heckewelder's Journey to the Wabash

https://archive.org/details/jstor-20083258/page/n1

October 12, 1792 - Heckeweller Party Reaches Clarksville

John Heckewelder's Journey to the Wabash

https://archive.org/details/jstor-20083258/page/n1

October 16, 1792 - Heckeweller Party Departs Fort Steuben

John Heckeweller's Journey to the Wabash

https://archive.org/details/jstor-20083258/page/n1

October 24, 1792 - Heckeweller Party Reaches Fort Washington

John Heckewelder's Journey to the Wabash

https://archive.org/details/jstor-20083258/page/n1

November 01, 1792 - Heckeweller Party Departs Fort Washington

John Heckewelder's Journey to the Wabash

https://archive.org/details/jstor-20083258/page/n1

http://wardepartmentpapers.org/document.php?id=7542

https://en.wikipedia.org/wiki/Northwest_Indian_War

November 03, 1792 - Little Turtle, Captures 3 Soldiers from Fort Hamilton

The History of Montgomery County, Ohio, Containing a History of the County https://books.google.com/books?id=mkLgWuNANpEC&pg=PA264&lpg=PA264&dq=att ack+fort+hamilton+november+3+1792&source=bl&ots=D4MUVNTuc2&sig=ACfU3U0Pr W56U5Xa36bYsDoXI2FHQNEe7Q&hl=en&sa=X&ved=2ahUKEwjkkb3GwbPhAhUGEawK HZhSD7cQ6AEwB3oECAYQAQ#v=onepage&q=attack%20fort%20hamilton%20november %203%201792&f=false

November 06, 1792 - Little Turtle Attacks Fort. St. Clair

https://en.wikipedia.org/wiki/Northwest_Indian_War
https://books.google.com/books?id=pW0zAQAAMAAJ&pg=PA335&lpg=PA3 35&dq=attack+fort+hamilton+november+3+1792&source=bl&ots=QZ1lqAaRKI&sig=ACf U3U0LVxQCSFPNYSrxTewGABXQ2-
Imjw&hl=en&sa=X&ved=2ahUKEwjkkb3GwbPhAhUGEawKHZhSD7cQ6AEwCXoECAc QAQ#v=onepage&q=attack%20fort%20hamilton%20november%203%201792&f=false
https://en.wikipedia.org/wiki/Fort_St._Clair

https://www.ohioexploration.com/miscellaneous/fortsaintclair/

November 09, 1792 - Advance Party Begins Clearing Legionville Site

https://en.wikipedia.org/wiki/Fort_Lafayette_(Pennsylvania)

https://www.timesonline.com/article/20150225/News/302259788

https://en.wikipedia.org/wiki/First_American_Regiment

https://en.wikipedia.org/wiki/Legionville

https://en.wikipedia.org/wiki/3rd_U.S._Infantry_Regiment_(The_Old_Guard)

https://armyhistory.org/the-battle-of-fallen-timbers-20-august-1794/

November 28, 1792 - General Wayne's Troops Arrive at Legionville

https://en.wikipedia.org/wiki/Legionville

https://armyhistory.org/the-battle-of-fallen-timbers-20-august-1794/

William Henry Harrison and the Conquest of the Ohio Country: Frontier ...

By David Curtis Skaggs

https://books.google.com/books?id=nWzeAgAAQBAJ&pg=PA26&lpg=PA26&dq=wilkin son+fort+jefferson+january+1792&source=bl&ots=sWBehp96Pb&sig=7BBJ8kNNlUIIKprE PiKTu0eI7mY&hl=en&sa=X&ved=2ahUKEwiNnb-h6qveAhXK34MKHUP7B-
QQ6AEwAnoECAcQAQ#v=onepage&q=wilkinson%20fort%20jefferson%20january%2017 92&f=false

https://www.timesonline.com/article/20150225/News/302259788

Early December 1792 - Wayne's Army Completes Building Living Quarters - Training Resumes

https://en.wikipedia.org/wiki/Buck_and_ball

https://armyhistory.org/the-battle-of-fallen-timbers-20-august-1794/
https://books.google.com/books?id=nWzeAgAAQBAJ&pg=PA26&lpg=PA26&dq=wilkinson+fort+jefferson+january+1792&source=bl&ots=sWBehp96Pb&sig=7BBJ8kNNlUIIKprEPiKTu0eI7mY&hl=en&sa=X&ved=2ahUKEwiNnb-h6qveAhXK34MKHUP7B-QQ6AEwAnoECAcQAQ#v=onepage&q=wilkinson%20fort%20jefferson%20january%2017 92&f=false

http://www.nps.gov/vafo/historyculture/vonsteuben.htm

http://www.ushistory.org/valleyforge/served/steuben.html

http://en.wikipedia.org/wiki/Friedrich_Wilhelm_von_Steuben

http://www.history.com/this-day-in-history/friedrich-von-steuben-arrives-at-valley-forge

The Battle Of The Wabash And The Battle Of Fort Recovery:

Christine K. Thompson, Principal Investigator

Erin A. Steinwachs

Kevin C. Nolan, Co-Principal Investigator

https://www.bsu.edu/-/media/www/departmentalcontent/aal/aalpdfs/abpp%20composite%20map%20docum ent%20final.pdf?la=en

Early March, 1793 - Indian Chiefs Visit Legionville to Discuss Terms for Peace

Graham's Illustrated Magazine of Literature, Romance, Art, and Fashion, Volume 5

edited by George R. Graham, Edgar Allan Poe

https://books.google.com/books?id=O00yAQAAMAAJ&pg=PA111&lpg=PA111&dq=ind ian+chiefs+meet+legionville+1793+march&source=bl&ots=DVRHbGVj3d&sig=ACfU3U2B cq7xGJMpqPePBB5ozPlnmC5c9A&hl=en&sa=X&ved=2ahUKEwjyqcuhr9HhAhUD5awKH QDUDacQ6AEwCnoECAYQAQ#v=onepage&q=indian%20chiefs%20meet%20legionville %201793%20march&f=false

https://en.wikipedia.org/wiki/Legionville

https://armyhistory.org/the-battle-of-fallen-timbers-20-august-1794/

William Henry Harrison and the Conquest of the Ohio Country: Frontier ...

By David Curtis Skaggs

April 30, 1793 - Legion of the United States Departs Legionville

https://books.google.com/books?id=nWzeAgAAQBAJ&pg=PA26&lpg=PA26&dq=wilkin son+fort+jefferson+january+1792&source=bl&ots=sWBehp96Pb&sig=7BBJ8kNNlUIIKprE PiKTu0eI7mY&hl=en&sa=X&ved=2ahUKEwiNnb-h6qveAhXK34MKHUP7B-QQ6AEwAnoECAcQAQ#v=onepage&q=wilkinson%20fort%20jefferson%20january%2017 92&f=false

https://www.timesonline.com/article/20150225/News/302259788

Fallen Timbers 1794: The US Army's first victory

By John F. Winkler

https://books.google.com/books?id=hFmbCwAAQBAJ&pg=PA38&lpg=PA38&dq=legion ville+april+30+1793&source=bl&ots=BwcYHgkwPs&sig=ACfU3U1oM7j0z3YW1zbcCDwy lUUuNfHDag&hl=en&sa=X&ved=2ahUKEwjxlKGB9dbhAhUHRK0KHXduDPgQ6AEwBn oECAYQAQ#v=onepage&q=legionville%20april%2030%201793&f=false

May 05, 1793 - Legion of the United States Arrives Fort Washington

https://www.nkytribune.com/2018/04/our-rich-history-appearance-of-a-town-of-some-respectability-part-two-on-18th-century-cincinnati/

Fallen Timbers 1794: The US Army's first victory

By John F. Winkler

https://books.google.com/books?id=hFmbCwAAQBAJ&pg=PA38&lpg=PA38&dq=legion ville+april+30+1793&source=bl&ots=BwcYHgkwPs&sig=ACfU3U1oM7j0z3YW1zbcCDwy lUUuNfHDag&hl=en&sa=X&ved=2ahUKEwjxlKGB9dbhAhUHRK0KHXduDPgQ6AEwBn oECAYQAQ#v=onepage&q=legionville%20april%2030%201793&f=false

Mid May, 1793 - Joseph Brandt Meets with John Graves Simcoe

http://parkscanadahistory.com/series/chs/14/chs14-1g.htm

https://www.findagrave.com/memorial/8878/john-graves-simcoe

https://en.wikipedia.org/wiki/John_Graves_Simcoe

John Graves Simcoe (February 25, 1752 – October 26, 1806)

https://www.findagrave.com/memorial/8878/john-graves-simcoe

https://en.wikipedia.org/wiki/John_Graves_Simcoe

https://www.thefamouspeople.com/profiles/john-graves-simcoe-16297.php

May 24, 1793 - Wayne Sends Reinforcements to Fort Jefferson

Fallen Timbers 1794: The US Army's first victory

By John F. Winkler

https://books.google.com/books?id=hFmbCwAAQBAJ&pg=PA38&lpg=PA38&dq=legion ville+april+30+1793&source=bl&ots=BwcYHgkwPs&sig=ACfU3U1oM7j0z3YW1zbcCDwy lUUuNfHDag&hl=en&sa=X&ved=2ahUKEwjxlKGB9dbhAhUHRK0KHXduDPgQ6AEwBn oECAYQAQ#v=onepage&q=legionville%20april%2030%201793&f=false

June 06, 1793 - Indian Attacks Near Fort Hamilton

Fallen Timbers 1794: The US Army's first victory

By John F. Winkler

https://books.google.com/books?id=hFmbCwAAQBAJ&pg=PA38&lpg=PA38&dq=legion ville+april+30+1793&source=bl&ots=BwcYHgkwPs&sig=ACfU3U1oM7j0z3YW1zbcCDwy

lUUuNfHDag&hl=en&sa=X&ved=2ahUKEwjxlKGB9dbhAhUHRK0KHXduDPgQ6AEwBn
oECAYQAQ#v=onepage&q=legionville%20april%2030%201793&f=false

July 07, 1793 - Indian Delegation Meets with Commissioners

American State Papers: Documents, Legislative and Executive, of the Congress ...

By United States. Congress

https://books.google.com/books?id=hbWsTT4Mdr0C&pg=PA345&lpg=PA345&dq=corn
planter+lincoln+niagara+july+7+1793&source=bl&ots=WZ3nQNeq6X&sig=ACfU3U3chN
HsL5JE5ZvvLvAD51ysdLLYHA&hl=en&sa=X&ved=2ahUKEwjZ5LbFi_rhAhUOKawKHf
q9BRcQ6AEwDnoECAcQAQ#v=onepage&q=cornplanter%20lincoln%20niagara%20july%
207%201793&f=false

http://parkscanadahistory.com/series/chs/14/chs14-1g.htm

Late July 1793 - Brandt Meets With Indians at Sandusky

http://parkscanadahistory.com/series/chs/14/chs14-1g.htm

https://books.google.com/books?id=hbWsTT4Mdr0C&pg=PA345&lpg=PA345&dq=corn
planter+lincoln+niagara+july+7+1793&source=bl&ots=WZ3nQNeq6X&sig=ACfU3U3chN
HsL5JE5ZvvLvAD51ysdLLYHA&hl=en&sa=X&ved=2ahUKEwjZ5LbFi_rhAhUOKawKHf
q9BRcQ6AEwDnoECAcQAQ#v=onepage&q=cornplanter%20lincoln%20niagara%20july%
207%201793&f=false

July 10, 1793 - William Wells Reaches Indian Council

https://books.google.com/books?id=hFmbCwAAQBAJ&pg=PA38&lpg=PA38&dq=legion
ville+april+30+1793&source=bl&ots=BwcYHgkwPs&sig=ACfU3U1oM7j0z3YW1zbcCDwy
lUUuNfHDag&hl=en&sa=X&ved=2ahUKEwjxlKGB9dbhAhUHRK0KHXduDPgQ6AEwBn
oECAYQAQ#v=onepage&q=legionville%20april%2030%201793&f=false

July 31, 1793 - Grand Council Meets with United States Commissioners

https://en.wikipedia.org/wiki/Northwest_Indian_War#Council_on_the_Auglaize

Fallen Timbers 1794: The US Army's first victory

By John F. Winkler

https://books.google.com/books?id=hFmbCwAAQBAJ&pg=PA38&lpg=PA38&dq=legion
ville+april+30+1793&source=bl&ots=BwcYHgkwPs&sig=ACfU3U1oM7j0z3YW1zbcCDwy
lUUuNfHDag&hl=en&sa=X&ved=2ahUKEwjxlKGB9dbhAhUHRK0KHXduDPgQ6AEwBn
oECAYQAQ#v=onepage&q=legionville%20april%2030%201793&f=false

http://parkscanadahistory.com/series/chs/14/chs14-1g.htm

American State Papers: Documents, Legislative and Executive, of the Congress ...

By United States. Congress

https://books.google.com/books?id=hbWsTT4Mdr0C&pg=PA345&lpg=PA345&dq=corn
planter+lincoln+niagara+july+7+1793&source=bl&ots=WZ3nQNeq6X&sig=ACfU3U3chN
HsL5JE5ZvvLvAD51ysdLLYHA&hl=en&sa=X&ved=2ahUKEwjZ5LbFi_rhAhUOKawKHf

q9BRcQ6AEwDnoECAcQAQ#v=onepage&q=cornplanter%20lincoln%20niagara%20july%
207%201793&f=false

August 25, 1793 - General Wayne Issues Marching Orders

William Henry Harrison and the Conquest of the Ohio Country: Frontier ...

By David Curtis Skaggs

https://books.google.com/books?id=nWzeAgAAQBAJ&pg=PA26&lpg=PA26&dq=wilkin
son+fort+jefferson+january+1792&source=bl&ots=sWBehp96Pb&sig=7BBJ8kNNlUIIKprE
PiKTu0eI7mY&hl=en&sa=X&ved=2ahUKEwiNnb-h6qveAhXK34MKHUP7B-
QQ6AEwAnoECAcQAQ#v=onepage&q=wilkinson%20fort%20jefferson%20january%2017
92&f=false

Michigan Historical Collections, General Wayne's Orderly Book - Page 491

September 16, 1793 - William Wells Delivers Report to General Wayne

https://books.google.com/books?id=pipKAQAAMAAJ&pg=PA533&lpg=PA533&dq=%2
2order+of+battle%22+august+25+1793+general+wayne&source=bl&ots=zJBU8NZvg_&sig
=ACfU3U2jzPSunBVIo86b3_vMEbbxWMzciw&hl=en&sa=X&ved=2ahUKEwii8qTg0oviAh
UMcq0KHeOWBxcQ6AEwBHoECAkQAQ#v=onepage&q=%22order%20of%20battle%22
%20august%2025%201793%20general%20wayne&f=false

https://scholarworks.iu.edu/journals/index.php/imh/article/view/8727
        https://drloihjournal.blogspot.com/2018/07/william-wells-miami-indian-
fights-for-US-in-fort-dearborn-battle.html

October 07, 1793 - Wayne Begins March North

McCarty's Annual Statistician, Volume 6, Part 1882

https://books.google.com/books?id=wHoZAAAAYAAJ&pg=PA257&lpg=PA257&dq=sc
ott+joins+wayne+1793&source=bl&ots=9tAwwtv2Ui&sig=ACfU3U1o9fKifxAITePdyf0Ov
KpihEvOcQ&hl=en&sa=X&ved=2ahUKEwjG5pqy4ZDiAhVJY6wKHa_oDn0Q6AEwCnoE
CAYQAQ#v=onepage&q=scott%20joins%20wayne%201793&f=false

Michigan Historical Collections - General Wayne's Orderly Book - Page 491

Unlikely General: "Mad" Anthony Wayne and the Battle for America

By Mary Stockwell

https://books.google.com/books?id=Xb1TDwAAQBAJ&pg=PA180&lpg=PA180&dq=way
ne+hobsons+choice+october+7&source=bl&ots=x-
YG6r9Gh_&sig=ACfU3U0IXSdb3zj2rYkBBiikyo-
Hb6ux6A&hl=en&sa=X&ved=2ahUKEwiv68mo5pDiAhVFKawKHUizCFgQ6AEwA3oEC
AkQAQ#v=onepage&q=wayne%20hobsons%20choice%20october%207&f=false

Anthony Wayne, Soldier of the Early Republic

By Paul David Nelson, Paul Nelson

https://books.google.com/books?id=qiF5OnyClVUC&pg=PA245&lpg=PA245&dq=wayn
e+hobsons+choice+october+7&source=bl&ots=UEgpR2R7DH&sig=ACfU3U3InrSE2123oe
phmRqWJagivmwr8w&hl=en&sa=X&ved=2ahUKEwiv68mo5pDiAhVFKawKHUizCFgQ6
AEwAHoECAIQAQ#v=onepage&q=wayne%20hobsons%20choice%20october%207&f=fals
e

Historic Highways of America: Volume 8: Military Roads of the Mississippi Basin

By Archer Butler Hulbert

https://books.google.com/books?id=PQ5BDwAAQBAJ&pg=PA59&lpg=PA59&dq=wayn
e+hobsons+choice+october+7&source=bl&ots=NwrYkS8JuS&sig=ACfU3U0VEHdlg5RgQq
9Z_q4CpwXr4pk0pw&hl=en&sa=X&ved=2ahUKEwiv68mo5pDiAhVFKawKHUizCFgQ6
AEwBXoECAUQAQ#v=onepage&q=wayne%20hobsons%20choice%20october%207&f=fal
se

October 08, 1793 - Wayne's Forces Reach Fort Hamilton

By Archer Butler Hulbert

https://books.google.com/books?id=PQ5BDwAAQBAJ&pg=PA59&lpg=PA59&dq=wayn
e+hobsons+choice+october+7&source=bl&ots=NwrYkS8JuS&sig=ACfU3U0VEHdlg5RgQq
9Z_q4CpwXr4pk0pw&hl=en&sa=X&ved=2ahUKEwiv68mo5pDiAhVFKawKHUizCFgQ6
AEwBXoECAUQAQ#v=onepage&q=wayne%20hobsons%20choice%20october%207&f=fal
se

Historic Highways of America: Volume 8: Military Roads of the Mississippi Basin

By Archer Butler Hulbert

https://books.google.com/books?id=H283AQAAMAAJ&pg=PA894&lpg=PA894&dq=wa
yne+hobsons+choice+october+7&source=bl&ots=LT4xVJCfeE&sig=ACfU3U3CjfqdFLsu9N
Lv616TOYALZUXvkg&hl=en&sa=X&ved=2ahUKEwiv68mo5pDiAhVFKawKHUizCFgQ6
AEwAXoECAYQAQ#v=onepage&q=wayne%20hobsons%20choice%20october%207&f=fal
se

https://piquaoh.org/location/history/general-anthony-wayne/

October 13, 1793 - Wayne Camps at Future Fort Greenville

https://books.google.com/books?id=wHoZAAAAYAAJ&pg=PA257&lpg=PA257&dq=sc
ott+joins+wayne+1793&source=bl&ots=9tAwwtv2Ui&sig=ACfU3U1o9fKifxAITePdyf0Ov
KpihEvOcQ&hl=en&sa=X&ved=2ahUKEwjG5pqy4ZDiAhVJY6wKHa_oDn0Q6AEwCnoE
CAYQAQ#v=onepage&q=scott%20joins%20wayne%201793&f=false

https://books.google.com/books?id=U4MUAAAAYAAJ&pg=PA210&lpg=PA210&dq=fo
rt+greenville+october+1793&source=bl&ots=ZEOp_i0R3v&sig=ACfU3U03of7oFc6P9dBEX
weHgMsWU1dfKw&hl=en&sa=X&ved=2ahUKEwjEoaGS1ZriAhVDiqwKHcarD-
UQ6AEwBnoECAYQAQ#v=onepage&q=fort%20greenville%20october%201793&f=false

https://journals.psu.edu/pmhb/article/viewFile/40939/40660

October 17, 1793 - Natives Attack Supply Wagon ConvoyQuartermaster support of the
Army: a history of the corps, 1775-1939

By Erna Risch

https://books.google.com/books?id=7FH3wb1DqNIC&pg=PA108&lpg=PA108&dq=shaylor+october+1793+supplies+attacked&source=bl&ots=qsMYMCx8nR&sig=ACfU3U2jwooEb9gVhfM2oMrnX_yFaLZeHA&hl=en&sa=X&ved=2ahUKEwiM7beEq53iAhXSmq0KHRz2DEAQ6AEwAnoECAgQAQ#v=onepage&q=shaylor%20october%201793%20supplies%20attacked&f=false

https://journals.psu.edu/pmhb/article/viewFile/40939/40660

The Soldiers of America's First Army, 1791

By Richard M. Lytle

https://books.google.com/books?id=UDxBU0JfgjMC&pg=PA212&lpg=PA212&dq=commander+fort.+St.+Clair+1792&source=bl&ots=4pmgInuBW6&sig=hmR9N4MQbMiYINeDaY9im2T2Ltc&hl=en&sa=X&ved=2ahUKEwiO0ey0ifLfAhWE2YMKHbxcC2cQ6AEwCHoECAEQAQ#v=onepage&q&f=false

November 21, 1793 - Wayne's Forces Begin Construction of Fort Greene

http://www.garstmuseum.org/darke-county-history

http://dailyadvocate.com/news/8125/222-years-ago-gen-anthony-wayne-ordered-construction-of-fort-greene-ville

https://armyhistory.org/the-battle-of-fallen-timbers-20-august-1794/

https://books.google.com/books?id=sApvBAAAQBAJ&pg=PA226&lpg=PA226&dq=greenville+july+28+1794&source=bl&ots=abqMRa-Z8b&sig=lL_wKLJ1P9WRd2SIDlGm_JekjBo&hl=en&sa=X&ved=0ahUKEwi8lcmZ7orUAhXK7IMKHfGsBk8Q6AEIMDAC#v=onepage&q=greenville%20july%2028%201794&f=false

https://www.dailyadvocate.com/news/8125/222-years-ago-gen-anthony-wayne-ordered-construction-of-fort-greene-ville

https://www.dailyadvocate.com/news/72145/1793-drawing-of-ft-greene-ville-found
https://journals.psu.edu/pmhb/article/viewFile/40939/40660

December 12, 1793 - Wayne Dispatches Force to Site of St. Claire's Defeat

http://touringohio.com/history/fort-recovery.html

Ohio Historic Places Dictionary, Volume 2

By Editorial Staff, State History Publications, LLC

https://books.google.com/books?id=YfvhVln0D20C&pg=PA991&lpg=PA991&dq=fort+recovery+march+1794&source=bl&ots=kxlissF2ck&sig=ACfU3U0ScLneC59U5nuuWH6SP4K1MJSdVQ&hl=en&sa=X&ved=2ahUKEwjqjs2rurHiAhULPa0KHWSkDo84ChDoATAOegQIAxAB#v=onepage&q=fort%20recovery%20march%201794&f=false

December 25, 1793 - Wayne's Forces Reach Site of St. Claire's Defeat

http://www.garstmuseum.org/darke-county-history

http://dailyadvocate.com/news/8125/222-years-ago-gen-anthony-wayne-ordered-construction-of-fort-greene-ville

https://armyhistory.org/the-battle-of-fallen-timbers-20-august-1794/

https://books.google.com/books?id=sApvBAAAQBAJ&pg=PA226&lpg=PA226&dq=greenville+july+28+1794&source=bl&ots=abqMRa-Z8b&sig=IL_wKLJ1P9WRd2SIDlGm_JekjBo&hl=en&sa=X&ved=0ahUKEwi8lcmZ7orUAhXK7IMKHfGsBk8Q6AEIMDAC#v=onepage&q=greenville%20july%2028%201794&f=false

http://history.rays-place.com/oh/mer-f-recovery.htm

http://touringohio.com/history/fort-recovery.html

January 15, 1794 - Indiana Governor Noah Noble Born

https://en.wikipedia.org/wiki/Noah_Noble

http://www.in.gov/history/2742.htm

http://www.nga.org/cms/home/governors/past-governors-bios/page_indiana/col2-content/main-content-list/title_noble_noah.html

https://en.wikipedia.org/wiki/Whig_Party_(United_States)

February 19, 1794 - James Brown Ray - Indiana Governor (1794-1848)

http://www.in.gov/history/2743.htm

https://en.wikipedia.org/wiki/James_B._Ray

Early March 1794 - Fort Recovery Complete

Ohio Historic Places Dictionary, Volume 2

By Editorial Staff, State History Publications, LLC

https://books.google.com/books?id=YfvhVln0D20C&pg=PA991&lpg=PA991&dq=fort+recovery+march+1794&source=bl&ots=kxlissF2ck&sig=ACfU3U0ScLneC59U5nuuWH6SP4K1MJSdVQ&hl=en&sa=X&ved=2ahUKEwjqjs2rurHiAhULPa0KHWSkDo84ChDoATAOegQIAxAB#v=onepage&q=fort%20recovery%20march%201794&f=false

http://touringohio.com/history/fort-recovery.html

April 1794 - Land Office Virginia Military District Opens

https://hcgsohio.org/cpage.php?pt=76

https://en.wikipedia.org/wiki/Virginia_Military_District

https://hcgsohio.org/cpage.php?pt=66

http://www.ohiohistorycentral.org/w/Virginia_Military_District

June 29, 1794 - Convoy Departs Fort Greenville For Fort Recovery

https://www.bsu.edu/-
/media/www/departmentalcontent/aal/aalpdfs/abpp%20composite%20map%20docum
ent%20final.pdf?la=en

June 29, 1794 - British and Indian Force Arrive at Fort Recovery

https://www.bsu.edu/-
/media/www/departmentalcontent/aal/aalpdfs/abpp%20composite%20map%20docum
ent%20final.pdf?la=en

https://www.wikiwand.com/en/Northwest_Indian_War

https://en.wikipedia.org/wiki/Northwest_Indian_War

https://books.google.com/books?id=YfvhVln0D20C&pg=PA991&lpg=PA991&dq=fort+re
covery+march+1794&source=bl&ots=kxlissF2ck&sig=ACfU3U0ScLneC59U5nuuWH6SP4K
1MJSdVQ&hl=en&sa=X&ved=2ahUKEwjqjs2rurHiAhULPa0KHWSkDo84ChDoATAOegQ
IAxAB#v=onepage&q=fort%20recovery%20march%201794&f=false

https://www.flickr.com/photos/hystericalmark/5819994974
https://en.wikipedia.org/wiki/Fort_Recovery

http://www.fortrecoverymuseum.com/history

https://military.wikia.org/wiki/Fort_Recovery

http://genealogytrails.com/ind/wells/williamwellsbio.html

June 30, 1794 - Little Turtle Attacks Fort Recovery Supply Train

https://books.google.com/books?id=YfvhVln0D20C&pg=PA991&lpg=PA991&dq=fort+re
covery+march+1794&source=bl&ots=kxlissF2ck&sig=ACfU3U0ScLneC59U5nuuWH6SP4K
1MJSdVQ&hl=en&sa=X&ved=2ahUKEwjqjs2rurHiAhULPa0KHWSkDo84ChDoATAOegQ
IAxAB#v=onepage&q=fort%20recovery%20march%201794&f=false

http://touringohio.com/history/fort-recovery.html   https://www.bsu.edu/-
/media/www/departmentalcontent/aal/aalpdfs/abpp%20composite%20map%20docum
ent%20final.pdf?la=en

https://en.wikipedia.org/wiki/Fort_Recovery

http://www.fortrecoverymuseum.com/history

July 01, 1794 - Battle of Fort Recovery

https://books.google.com/books?id=YfvhVln0D20C&pg=PA991&lpg=PA991&dq=fort+re
covery+march+1794&source=bl&ots=kxlissF2ck&sig=ACfU3U0ScLneC59U5nuuWH6SP4K
1MJSdVQ&hl=en&sa=X&ved=2ahUKEwjqjs2rurHiAhULPa0KHWSkDo84ChDoATAOegQ
IAxAB#v=onepage&q=fort%20recovery%20march%201794&f=false

http://touringohio.com/history/fort-recovery.html

https://en.wikipedia.org/wiki/Northwest_Indian_War

July 28, 1794 - General Wayne Begins March from Greenville

Paul R. Wonning

The Encyclopedia of the Wars of the Early American Republic, 1783–1812: A ...

edited by Spencer C. Tucker

https://books.google.com/books?id=sApvBAAAQBAJ&pg=PA226&lpg=PA226&dq=gree
nville+july+28+1794&source=bl&ots=abqMRa-
Z8b&sig=lL_wKLJ1P9WRd2SIDlGm_JekjBo&hl=en&sa=X&ved=0ahUKEwi8lcmZ7orUAh
XK7IMKHfGsBk8Q6AEIMDAC#v=onepage&q=greenville%20july%2028%201794&f=false

History of Van Wert and Mercer Counties, Ohio

https://books.google.com/books?id=W_Cqb5YSQ1IC&pg=PA55&lpg=PA55&dq=fort+rec
overy+finished+march+1794&source=bl&ots=GJpRainkXg&sig=ACfU3U1tDsMSLE1rsb2v
05h8UVPW4mhXnw&hl=en&sa=X&ved=2ahUKEwiQpoCPx8DiAhUGd6wKHTZYATo4C
hDoATALegQIBRAB#v=onepage&q=fort%20recovery%20finished%20march%201794&f=f
alse

William Clark's Journal of General Wayne's Campaign

https://www.americanantiquarian.org/proceedings/44524998.pdf

A Precise Journal of General Wayne's Campaign

https://www.americanantiquarian.org/proceedings/44524998.pdf

The Encyclopedia of the Wars of the Early American Republic, 1783–1812: A ...

edited by Spencer C. Tucker

https://books.google.com/books?id=sApvBAAAQBAJ&pg=PA226&lpg=PA226&dq=gree
nville+july+28+1794&source=bl&ots=abqMRa-
Z8b&sig=lL_wKLJ1P9WRd2SIDlGm_JekjBo&hl=en&sa=X&ved=0ahUKEwi8lcmZ7orUAh
XK7IMKHfGsBk8Q6AEIMDAC#v=onepage&q=greenville%20july%2028%201794&f=false

July 28, 1794 - General Wayne Begins March from Greenville

History of Van Wert and Mercer Counties, Ohio

https://books.google.com/books?id=W_Cqb5YSQ1IC&pg=PA55&lpg=PA55&dq=fort+rec
overy+finished+march+1794&source=bl&ots=GJpRainkXg&sig=ACfU3U1tDsMSLE1rsb2v
05h8UVPW4mhXnw&hl=en&sa=X&ved=2ahUKEwiQpoCPx8DiAhUGd6wKHTZYATo4C
hDoATALegQIBRAB#v=onepage&q=fort%20recovery%20finished%20march%201794&f=f
alse

William Clark's Journal of General Wayne's Campaign

https://www.americanantiquarian.org/proceedings/44524998.pdf

A Precise Journal of General Wayne's Campaign

https://www.americanantiquarian.org/proceedings/44524998.pdf

The Encyclopedia of the Wars of the Early American Republic, 1783–1812: A ...

edited by Spencer C. Tucker

https://books.google.com/books?id=sApvBAAAQBAJ&pg=PA226&lpg=PA226&dq=gree
nville+july+28+1794&source=bl&ots=abqMRa-
Z8b&sig=IL_wKLJ1P9WRd2SIDlGm_JekjBo&hl=en&sa=X&ved=0ahUKEwi8lcmZ7orUAh
XK7IMKHfGsBk8Q6AEIMDAC#v=onepage&q=greenville%20july%2028%201794&f=false

July 29, 1794 - Wayne's Army Reaches Fort Recovery

History of Van Wert and Mercer Counties, Ohio

https://books.google.com/books?id=W_Cqb5YSQ1IC&pg=PA55&lpg=PA55&dq=fort+rec
overy+finished+march+1794&source=bl&ots=GJpRainkXg&sig=ACfU3U1tDsMSLE1rsb2v
05h8UVPW4mhXnw&hl=en&sa=X&ved=2ahUKEwiQpoCPx8DiAhUGd6wKHTZYATo4C
hDoATALegQIBRAB#v=onepage&q=fort%20recovery%20finished%20march%201794&f=f
alse

William Clark's Journal of General Wayne's Campaign

https://www.americanantiquarian.org/proceedings/44524998.pdf

A Precise Journal of General Wayne's Campaign

https://www.americanantiquarian.org/proceedings/44524998.pdf

July 31, 1794 – Wayne's Troops Halt to Build Bridge over Beaver Creek

William Clark's Journal of General Wayne's Campaign

https://www.americanantiquarian.org/proceedings/44524998.pdf

A Precise Journal of General Wayne's Campaign

https://www.americanantiquarian.org/proceedings/44524998.pdf

Lieutenant John Boyer's A Journal of General Wayne's Campaign

http://www.toledosattic.org/images/pdfs/nwoq-by-issue/NWOQ_1929_Vol1-2.pdf

August 01, 1794 - Wayne's Troops Reach St. Mary's River

William Clark's Journal of General Wayne's Campaign

https://www.americanantiquarian.org/proceedings/44524998.pdf

A Precise Journal of General Wayne's Campaign

https://www.americanantiquarian.org/proceedings/44524998.pdf

Lieutenant John Boyer's A Journal of General Wayne's Campaign

http://www.toledosattic.org/images/pdfs/nwoq-by-issue/NWOQ_1929_Vol1-2.pdf

August 02, 3, 1794 - Army In Camp

William Clark's Journal of General Wayne's Campaign

https://www.americanantiquarian.org/proceedings/44524998.pdf

A Precise Journal of General Wayne's Campaign

https://www.americanantiquarian.org/proceedings/44524998.pdf

Lieutenant John Boyer's A Journal of General Wayne's Campaign

http://www.toledosattic.org/images/pdfs/nwoq-by-issue/NWOQ_1929_Vol1-2.pdf

August 07, 1794 - Wayne's Troops Reach Au Glaize River

William Clark's Journal of General Wayne's Campaign

https://www.americanantiquarian.org/proceedings/44524998.pdf

A Precise Journal of General Wayne's Campaign

https://www.americanantiquarian.org/proceedings/44524998.pdf

Lieutenant John Boyer's A Journal of General Wayne's Campaign

http://www.toledosattic.org/images/pdfs/nwoq-by-issue/NWOQ_1929_Vol1-2.pdf

August 08, 1794 - Wayne's Troops Occupy Amerindian Headquarters

William Clark's Journal of General Wayne's Campaign

https://www.americanantiquarian.org/proceedings/44524998.pdf

A Precise Journal of General Wayne's Campaign

https://www.americanantiquarian.org/proceedings/44524998.pdf

Lieutenant John Boyer's A Journal of General Wayne's Campaign

http://www.toledosattic.org/images/pdfs/nwoq-by-issue/NWOQ_1929_Vol1-2.pdf

August 09, 1794 - General Wayne's Troops Begin Building Fort

William Clark's Journal of General Wayne's Campaign

https://www.americanantiquarian.org/proceedings/44524998.pdf

A Precise Journal of General Wayne's Campaign

https://www.americanantiquarian.org/proceedings/44524998.pdf

Lieutenant John Boyer's A Journal of General Wayne's Campaign

http://www.toledosattic.org/images/pdfs/nwoq-by-issue/NWOQ_1929_Vol1-2.pdf

August 12, 1794 - William Wells and Robert McClellan Return with Prisoners

https://www.findagrave.com/memorial/10279165/christopher-bryan-miller

https://www.captainjacobvanmeterdar.org/the-story-of-christopher-miller-shawnee-adopted-son-march-program/

The History of Ohio, from Its Earliest Settlement to the Present Time

edited by William Henry Carpenter, Timothy Shay Arthur

https://books.google.com/books?id=vjkWAAAAYAAJ&pg=PA142&lpg=PA142&dq=henry+miller+scout+1794&source=bl&ots=u_ALmCldfm&sig=ACfU3U0luT6hhLUKm_Icusgu5jzjGh-QTw&hl=en&sa=X&ved=2ahUKEwia4e28h5bjAhXUX80KHasIDwgQ6AEwGHoECAkQAQ#v=onepage&q=henry%20miller%20scout%201794&f=false

The History of Ohio, from Its Earliest Settlement to the Present Time

edited by William Henry Carpenter, Timothy Shay Arthur

The Latimers: A Tale of the Western Insurrection of 1794

By Henry Christopher McCook

https://books.google.com/books?id=LJcpAAAAYAAJ&pg=PA309&lpg=PA309&dq=miller+scout+general+wayne+1794&source=bl&ots=WWw52gcLey&sig=ACfU3U0Tm3GMCow-5dygCzYxZHnz7T8x3A&hl=en&sa=X&ved=2ahUKEwj4xcOLhpbjAhWYXM0KHQuvDuAQ6AEwF3oECAoQAQ#v=onepage&q=miller%20scout%20general%20wayne%201794&f=false

Biographical and Historical Sketches: A Narrative of Hamilton and Its ...

By Stephen Decatur Cone

https://books.google.com/books?id=HjsVAAAAYAAJ&pg=PA40&lpg=PA40&dq=miller+scout+general+wayne+1794&source=bl&ots=XWUAZ2O8J6&sig=ACfU3U1BnBXuBcFH8K_7Mw6Sz297u4r8jg&hl=en&sa=X&ved=2ahUKEwi98aqFh5bjAhVLOs0KHe-sAgs4ChDoATABegQIBxAB#v=onepage&q=miller%20scout%20general%20wayne%201794&f=false

Christopher Bryan Miller (1768-1828)

The son of Ernest and Margaret Lindeman Miller, the family had migrated to Hardin County, Kentucky while Christopher and his brother Henry were children. The boys were captured by a band of Shawnee warriors in 1783. During their captivity, Christopher learned the Shawnee language as well as three other native tongues. In 1792 Henry escaped. Before he ran away, he tried in vain to convince Christopher to go with him.

Christopher remained with the Shawnee until captured by his brother Henry on August 12, 1794.

American State Papers: Documents, Legislative and ..., Volume 2; Volume 7

By United States. Congress

https://books.google.com/books?id=TfA1AQAAMAAJ&pg=PA490&lpg=PA490&dq=Chr istopher+Miller+miami+prisoner+1794&source=bl&ots=WaZHbYGTP0&sig=ACfU3U1v9h GX_jB29-4nl_A1vLjgCvp1dQ&hl=en&sa=X&ved=2ahUKEwjhk632gJbjAhXOKM0KHQz-Bz8Q6AEwBnoECAkQAQ#v=onepage&q=Christopher%20Miller%20miami%20prisoner%201794&f=false

Annals of the West: Embracing a Concise Account of Principal Events, which ...

By James Handasyd Perkins

https://books.google.com/books?id=f0gVAAAAYAAJ&pg=PA434&lpg=PA434&dq=Chri stopher+Miller+miami+prisoner+1794&source=bl&ots=SfLOjy1Vw5&sig=ACfU3U3Q8-wIxlADJzqqQfvyAZbT5pkx1Q&hl=en&sa=X&ved=2ahUKEwjhk632gJbjAhXOKM0KHQz-Bz8Q6AEwC3oECAgQAQ#v=onepage&q=Christopher%20Miller%20miami%20prisoner%201794&f=false

William Clark's Journal of General Wayne's Campaign

https://www.americanantiquarian.org/proceedings/44524998.pdf

A Precise Journal of General Wayne's Campaign

https://www.americanantiquarian.org/proceedings/44524998.pdf

Lieutenant John Boyer's A Journal of General Wayne's Campaign

http://www.toledosattic.org/images/pdfs/nwoq-by-issue/NWOQ_1929_Vol1-2.pdf

August 13, 1794 - Wayne's Troops Complete Fort Defiance

Annals of the West: Embracing a Concise Account of Principal Events, which ...

By James Handasyd Perkins

https://books.google.com/books?id=f0gVAAAAYAAJ&pg=PA434&lpg=PA434&dq=Chri stopher+Miller+miami+prisoner+1794&source=bl&ots=SfLOjy1Vw5&sig=ACfU3U3Q8-wIxlADJzqqQfvyAZbT5pkx1Q&hl=en&sa=X&ved=2ahUKEwjhk632gJbjAhXOKM0KHQz-Bz8Q6AEwC3oECAgQAQ#v=onepage&q=Christopher%20Miller%20miami%20prisoner%201794&f=false

William Clark's Journal of General Wayne's Campaign

https://www.americanantiquarian.org/proceedings/44524998.pdf

A Precise Journal of General Wayne's Campaign

https://www.americanantiquarian.org/proceedings/44524998.pdf

Lieutenant John Boyer's A Journal of General Wayne's Campaign

http://www.toledosattic.org/images/pdfs/nwoq-by-issue/NWOQ_1929_Vol1-2.pdf

Mid August, 1794 - British Complete Fort Miamis

https://ss.sites.mtu.edu/mhugl/2017/10/19/fort-miami-oh/

http://www.ohiohistorycentral.org/w/Fort_Miamis

William Clark's Journal of General Wayne's Campaign

https://www.americanantiquarian.org/proceedings/44524998.pdf

A Precise Journal of General Wayne's Campaign

https://www.americanantiquarian.org/proceedings/44524998.pdf

Lieutenant John Boyer's A Journal of General Wayne's Campaign

http://www.toledosattic.org/images/pdfs/nwoq-by-issue/NWOQ_1929_Vol1-2.pdf

August 13, 1794 - Wayne Sends Miller Out with Letter Asking For Peace

The History of Ohio, from Its Earliest Settlement to the Present Time

edited by William Henry Carpenter, Timothy Shay Arthur

https://books.google.com/books?id=vjkWAAAAYAAJ&pg=PA142&lpg=PA142&dq=hen
ry+miller+scout+1794&source=bl&ots=u_ALmCldfm&sig=ACfU3U0luT6hhLUKm_Icusgu
5jzjGh-
QTw&hl=en&sa=X&ved=2ahUKEwia4e28h5bjAhXUX80KHasIDwgQ6AEwGHoECAkQA
Q#v=onepage&q=henry%20miller%20scout%201794&f=false

August 16, 1794 - Wayne Received Reply to His Appeal for Peace

William Clark's Journal of General Wayne's Campaign

https://www.americanantiquarian.org/proceedings/44524998.pdf

A Precise Journal of General Wayne's Campaign

https://www.americanantiquarian.org/proceedings/44524998.pdf

Lieutenant John Boyer's A Journal of General Wayne's Campaign

http://www.toledosattic.org/images/pdfs/nwoq-by-issue/NWOQ_1929_Vol1-2.pdf

August 18, 1794 - Wayne's Forces Reach Rocke De Bout

William Clark's Journal of General Wayne's Campaign

https://www.americanantiquarian.org/proceedings/44524998.pdf

A Precise Journal of General Wayne's Campaign

https://www.americanantiquarian.org/proceedings/44524998.pdf

Lieutenant John Boyer's A Journal of General Wayne's Campaign

http://www.toledosattic.org/images/pdfs/nwoq-by-issue/NWOQ_1929_Vol1-2.pdf

August 19, 1794 - Wayne Builds Fort Deposit

McCarty's Annual Statistician, Volume 6, Part 1882

https://books.google.com/books?id=wHoZAAAAYAAJ&pg=PA257&lpg=PA257&dq=sc
ott+joins+wayne+1793&source=bl&ots=9tAwwtv2Ui&sig=ACfU3U1o9fKifxAITePdyf0Ov
KpihEvOcQ&hl=en&sa=X&ved=2ahUKEwjG5pqy4ZDiAhVJY6wKHa_oDn0Q6AEwCnoE
CAYQAQ#v=onepage&q=scott%20joins%20wayne%201793&f=false

William Clark's Journal of General Wayne's Campaign

https://www.americanantiquarian.org/proceedings/44524998.pdf

A Precise Journal of General Wayne's Campaign

https://www.americanantiquarian.org/proceedings/44524998.pdf

Lieutenant John Boyer's A Journal of General Wayne's Campaign

http://www.toledosattic.org/images/pdfs/nwoq-by-issue/NWOQ_1929_Vol1-2.pdf

August 19, 1794   Indian Chiefs Hold Council - Prisoner Executed

https://books.google.com/books?id=MaoLLCcSIVYC&pg=PT1&lpg=PT1&dq=1793+harri
son+aide-de-
camp+wayne+june&source=bl&ots=TuEub1rjuD&sig=yWVbR3qtLJfvZevZaU1gTyv5tGI&
hl=en&sa=X&ved=2ahUKEwj4-
fb676bfAhWG4IMKHbqoCDkQ6AEwA3oECAkQAQ#v=onepage&q=1793%20harrison%2
0aide-de-camp%20wayne%20june&f=false

https://books.google.com/books?id=vjkWAAAAYAAJ&pg=PA142&lpg=PA142&dq=hen
ry+miller+scout+1794&source=bl&ots=u_ALmCldfm&sig=ACfU3U0luT6hhLUKm_Icusgu
5jzjGh-
QTw&hl=en&sa=X&ved=2ahUKEwia4e28h5bjAhXUX80KHasIDwgQ6AEwGHoECAkQA
Q#v=onepage&q=henry%20miller%20scout%201794&f=false

https://books.google.com/books?id=nWzeAgAAQBAJ&pg=PA26&lpg=PA26&dq=wilkin
son+fort+jefferson+january+1792&source=bl&ots=sWBehp96Pb&sig=7BBJ8kNNlUIIKprE
PiKTu0eI7mY&hl=en&sa=X&ved=2ahUKEwiNnb-h6qveAhXK34MKHUP7B-
QQ6AEwAnoECAcQAQ#v=onepage&q=wilkinson%20fort%20jefferson%20january%2017
92&f=false Page 39

https://books.google.com/books?id=vjkWAAAAYAAJ&pg=PA142&lpg=PA142&dq=hen
ry+miller+scout+1794&source=bl&ots=u_ALmCldfm&sig=ACfU3U0luT6hhLUKm_Icusgu
5jzjGh-
QTw&hl=en&sa=X&ved=2ahUKEwia4e28h5bjAhXUX80KHasIDwgQ6AEwGHoECAkQA
Q#v=onepage&q=henry%20miller%20scout%201794&f=false

https://books.google.com/books?id=MaoLLCcSIVYC&pg=PT1&lpg=PT1&dq=1793+harri
son+aide-de-
camp+wayne+june&source=bl&ots=TuEub1rjuD&sig=yWVbR3qtLJfvZevZaU1gTyv5tGI&
hl=en&sa=X&ved=2ahUKEwj4-
fb676bfAhWG4IMKHbqoCDkQ6AEwA3oECAkQAQ#v=onepage&q=1793%20harrison%2
0aide-de-camp%20wayne%20june&f=false

https://books.google.com/books?id=nWzeAgAAQBAJ&pg=PA26&lpg=PA26&dq=wilkin
son+fort+jefferson+january+1792&source=bl&ots=sWBehp96Pb&sig=7BBJ8kNNlUIIKprE
PiKTu0eI7mY&hl=en&sa=X&ved=2ahUKEwiNnb-h6qveAhXK34MKHUP7B-
QQ6AEwAnoECAcQAQ#v=onepage&q=wilkinson%20fort%20jefferson%20january%2017
92&f=false Page 39

https://books.google.com/books?id=nWzeAgAAQBAJ&pg=PA26&lpg=PA26&dq=wilkin
son+fort+jefferson+january+1792&source=bl&ots=sWBehp96Pb&sig=7BBJ8kNNlUIIKprE
PiKTu0eI7mY&hl=en&sa=X&ved=2ahUKEwiNnb-h6qveAhXK34MKHUP7B-
QQ6AEwAnoECAcQAQ#v=onepage&q=wilkinson%20fort%20jefferson%20january%2017
92&f=false Page 39

August 20, 1794 - Battle of Fallen Timbers

William Clark's Journal of General Wayne's Campaign

https://www.americanantiquarian.org/proceedings/44524998.pdf

A Precise Journal of General Wayne's Campaign

https://www.americanantiquarian.org/proceedings/44524998.pdf

Lieutenant John Boyer's A Journal of General Wayne's Campaign

http://www.toledosattic.org/images/pdfs/nwoq-by-issue/NWOQ_1929_Vol1-2.pdf

August 21, 1794 - Wayne's Remain Encamped at Fort Miamis

William Clark's Journal of General Wayne's Campaign

https://www.americanantiquarian.org/proceedings/44524998.pdf

A Precise Journal of General Wayne's Campaign

https://www.americanantiquarian.org/proceedings/44524998.pdf

Lieutenant John Boyer's A Journal of General Wayne's Campaign

http://www.toledosattic.org/images/pdfs/nwoq-by-issue/NWOQ_1929_Vol1-2.pdf

http://www.ohiohistorycentral.org/w/Fort_Miamis

August 22, 1794 - Wayne's Forces Pillage Area Around Fort Miamis

William Clark's Journal of General Wayne's Campaign

https://www.americanantiquarian.org/proceedings/44524998.pdf

A Precise Journal of General Wayne's Campaign

https://www.americanantiquarian.org/proceedings/44524998.pdf

Lieutenant John Boyer's A Journal of General Wayne's Campaign

http://www.toledosattic.org/images/pdfs/nwoq-by-issue/NWOQ_1929_Vol1-2.pdf

August 23, 1794 - Wayne's Troops Celebrate Their Victory, Honor the Dead

William Clark's Journal of General Wayne's Campaign

https://www.americanantiquarian.org/proceedings/44524998.pdf

A Precise Journal of General Wayne's Campaign

https://www.americanantiquarian.org/proceedings/44524998.pdf

Lieutenant John Boyer's A Journal of General Wayne's Campaign

http://www.toledosattic.org/images/pdfs/nwoq-by-issue/NWOQ_1929_Vol1-2.pdf

August 27, 1794 - Wayne's Troops Return to Fort Defiance

William Clark's Journal of General Wayne's Campaign

https://www.americanantiquarian.org/proceedings/44524998.pdf

A Precise Journal of General Wayne's Campaign

https://www.americanantiquarian.org/proceedings/44524998.pdf

Lieutenant John Boyer's A Journal of General Wayne's Campaign

http://www.toledosattic.org/images/pdfs/nwoq-by-issue/NWOQ_1929_Vol1-2.pdf

September 13, 1794 - Symmes Purchase

http://www.surveyhistory.org/symmes_purchase.htm

https://recordersoffice.hamilton-co.org/about_the_recorder/history_of_our_land.html

http://www.ohiohistorycentral.org/w/Land_Grants_and_Sales

September 17, 1794 - Legion of the United States Arrived at Kekionga

https://archfw.org/heritagetrail/centraldowntown/anthony-waynes-fort/

http://www.oocities.org/heartland/valley/7029/portage.html

http://egen.fortwayne.com/ns/projects/history/2000/roots/roots2.php

http://egen.fortwayne.com/ns/projects/history/haw20.php

September 19, 1794 - Ground Cleared for Construction of a Fort

William Clark's Journal of General Wayne's Campaign

https://www.americanantiquarian.org/proceedings/44524998.pdf

A Precise Journal of General Wayne's Campaign

https://www.americanantiquarian.org/proceedings/44524998.pdf

September 22, 1794 - Wayne Begins Construction of Fort Wayne

McCarty's Annual Statistician, Volume 6, Part 1882

https://books.google.com/books?id=wHoZAAAAYAAJ&pg=PA257&lpg=PA257&dq=sc
ott+joins+wayne+1793&source=bl&ots=9tAwwtv2Ui&sig=ACfU3U1o9fKifxAITePdyf0Ov
KpihEvOcQ&hl=en&sa=X&ved=2ahUKEwjG5pqy4ZDiAhVJY6wKHa_oDn0Q6AEwCnoE
CAYQAQ#v=onepage&q=scott%20joins%20wayne%201793&f=false

Annals of the West: Embracing a Concise Account of Principal Events, which ...

By James Handasyd Perkins

https://books.google.com/books?id=f0gVAAAAYAAJ&pg=PA434&lpg=PA434&dq=Chri
stopher+Miller+miami+prisoner+1794&source=bl&ots=SfLOjy1Vw5&sig=ACfU3U3Q8-
wIxlADJzqqQfvyAZbT5pkx1Q&hl=en&sa=X&ved=2ahUKEwjhk632gJbjAhXOKM0KHQz-
Bz8Q6AEwC3oECAgQAQ#v=onepage&q=Christopher%20Miller%20miami%20prisoner%
201794&f=false

https://archfw.org/heritagetrail/centraldowntown/anthony-waynes-fort/

William Clark's Journal of General Wayne's Campaign

https://www.americanantiquarian.org/proceedings/44524998.pdf

A Precise Journal of General Wayne's Campaign

https://www.americanantiquarian.org/proceedings/44524998.pdf

September 28, 1794 - Warriors Attack Party on Trail

William Clark's Journal of General Wayne's Campaign

https://www.americanantiquarian.org/proceedings/44524998.pdf

September 30, 1794 - Supplies Arrive at Camp
William Clark's Journal of General Wayne's Campaign
https://www.americanantiquarian.org/proceedings/44524998.pdf
A Precise Journal of General Wayne's Campaign
https://www.americanantiquarian.org/proceedings/44524998.pdf

October 02, 1794 Rebellion in the Camp
William Clark's Journal of General Wayne's Campaign
https://www.americanantiquarian.org/proceedings/44524998.pdf

William Clark's Journal of General Wayne's Campaign
https://www.americanantiquarian.org/proceedings/44524998.pdf

October 14, 1794 - General Scott's Volunteers Depart
A Precise Journal of General Wayne's Campaign
https://www.americanantiquarian.org/proceedings/44524998.pdf

October 24, 1794 - Lieutenant Colonel Hamtramck Takes Command
William Clark's Journal of General Wayne's Campaign
https://www.americanantiquarian.org/proceedings/44524998.pdf
A Precise Journal of General Wayne's Campaign
https://www.americanantiquarian.org/proceedings/44524998.pdf

October 26, 1794 - General Wayne's Troops Depart Fort Wayne
A Precise Journal of General Wayne's Campaign
https://www.americanantiquarian.org/proceedings/44524998.pdf
Map
Indiana
The Influence of the Indian Upon its History
E. Y. Guernsey
1932

November 02, 1794 - Wayne's Troops Return to Fort Greenville

https://archives.profsurv.com/magazine/article.aspx?i=1423

A Precise Journal of General Wayne's Campaign

https://www.americanantiquarian.org/proceedings/44524998.pdf

Joseph Brant (March 1742/3 - November 24, 1807)

https://www.geni.com/people/Chief-Joseph-Brant-Thayendanegea-of-the-Six-Nations/6000000003231034562

https://en.wikipedia.org/wiki/Joseph_Brant

http://www.josephbrant.com/

http://www.ohiohistorycentral.org/w/Joseph_Brant

https://books.google.com/books?id=hbWsTT4Mdr0C&pg=PA345&lpg=PA345&dq=corn
planter+lincoln+niagara+july+7+1793&source=bl&ots=WZ3nQNeq6X&sig=ACfU3U3chN
HsL5JE5ZvvLvAD51ysdLLYHA&hl=en&sa=X&ved=2ahUKEwjZ5LbFi_rhAhUOKawKHf
q9BRcQ6AEwDnoECAcQAQ#v=onepage&q=cornplanter%20lincoln%20niagara%20july%
207%201793&f=false

http://parkscanadahistory.com/series/chs/14/chs14-1g.htm

http://parkscanadahistory.com/series/chs/14/chs14-1g.htm

https://www.findagrave.com/memorial/8878/john-graves-simcoe

https://en.wikipedia.org/wiki/John_Graves_Simcoe

https://en.wikipedia.org/wiki/Northwest_Indian_War#Council_on_the_Auglaize

Fallen Timbers 1794: The US Army's first victory

By John F. Winkler

https://books.google.com/books?id=hFmbCwAAQBAJ&pg=PA38&lpg=PA38&dq=legion
ville+april+30+1793&source=bl&ots=BwcYHgkwPs&sig=ACfU3U1oM7j0z3YW1zbcCDwy
lUUuNfHDag&hl=en&sa=X&ved=2ahUKEwjxlKGB9dbhAhUHRK0KHXduDPgQ6AEwBn
oECAYQAQ#v=onepage&q=legionville%20april%2030%201793&f=false

http://parkscanadahistory.com/series/chs/14/chs14-1g.htm

https://books.google.com/books?id=hbWsTT4Mdr0C&pg=PA345&lpg=PA345&dq=corn
planter+lincoln+niagara+july+7+1793&source=bl&ots=WZ3nQNeq6X&sig=ACfU3U3chN
HsL5JE5ZvvLvAD51ysdLLYHA&hl=en&sa=X&ved=2ahUKEwjZ5LbFi_rhAhUOKawKHf
q9BRcQ6AEwDnoECAcQAQ#v=onepage&q=cornplanter%20lincoln%20niagara%20july%
207%201793&f=false

About the Author

Paul considers himself a bit of an Indiana hound, in that he likes to sniff out the interesting places and history of Indiana and use his books to tell people about them.

Join Paul on Facebook
https://www.facebook.com/Mossy-Feet-Books-474924602565571/
Twitter
https://twitter.com/MossyFeetBooks
mossyfeetbooks@gmail.com

Mossy Feet Books Catalog

To Get Your Free Copy of the Mossy Feet Books Catalogue, Click This Link.

http://mossyfeetbooks.blogspot.com/

Gardening Books

Fantasy Books

Humor

Science Fiction

Semi – Autobiographical Books

Travel Books

Sample Chapter 1
Indiana's Timeless Tales- 1795 – 1800
January 1795 - Native Leaders Gather at Fort Greenville

Sometime in mid to late January three influential Miami chiefs, including Pinšiwa or Jean Baptiste Richardville, and Blue Jacket, arrived at Fort Greenville to discuss peace terms.

Jean Baptiste Richardville (c. 1761 – August 13, 1841)

The son of French fur trader Joseph Drouet de Richardville and a Miami woman, Tacumwah Chief Richardville was a native of the Miami village of Kekionga. Kekionga was on the site of the present city of Fort Wayne. His mother was the sister of Miami chief Pacanne. His mother and sister were chiefs in the Miami tribe, a tribe that used a matrilineal system to trace family lines. A matrilineal system is a female based system. Chief Richardville gained his tribal status from his mother. His name, Pinšiwa, means Wildcat in the Miami language.

He received a good education, learning to speak four languages, English, Miami, Iroquois and French. He was a signer of both the 1818 Treaty of the Miami and the 1826 Treaty of Mississinwas. Though the Miami had lost control of the portage between the Maumee River and Little River as per the Treaty of Greenville in 1795, Richardville managed to acquire a trade license granting him a monopoly over the carry-over trade at the portage. The profits from this license and his acquisition of almost twenty square miles of property along the rivers made him one of the richest men in Indiana at his death in 1841. In 1827 he constructed the Richardville House in Fort Wayne, the first Greek Revival-style in that part of the state. Richardville tendered the use of his lands for the Miami tribe, which allowed almost half the tribe to remain in Indiana when the Federal Government removed the Amerindian from Indiana in 1846.

The Richardville home in Fort Wayne currently serves as a museum and interpretive center for Amerindian culture. It is the oldest Amerindian structure in the Midwest. Listed with

the National Historic Landmarks, the home is open to the public. For information, contact:
The History Center
302 East Berry Street
Fort Wayne, Indiana, 46802
260.426.2882 |
http://www.fwhistorycenter.com/chiefRichardvilleHouse.htmlMossy Feet Books
www.mossyfeetbooks.com